Quantum Kids: Guardians of AI

Story Quest and Activity Book

Angela Radcliffe

How Mighty We

This book is dedicated to the original innovators: The **parents**, the **mentors**, the **teachers** and the **stewards** of the next generation. As humanity sits awestruck by the breathtaking enormity of an artificial intelligence of our own making, may we always remember our **greatest inventions** are the sparks of imagination, wisdom, kindness, and empathy we imbue in the children under our guide.

Dear Young Seekers and Future AI Guardians,

Greetings! I'm Angela Radcliffe, a mom and the creator of "Quantum Kids: Guardians of AI." I'm excited to share this special book with you. It is a magical journey where creativity meets the fantastic world of Artificial Intelligence (AI). I want to tell you a little secret: I teamed up with AI at every step in making this book. AI helped me write this book and design fun activities. It even created the picture on the cover, turning my imagination into the book you now hold. If it can help me create a whole story and activity book, imagine what you can do after reading it!

I first had an opportunity to use AI in my job about ten years ago, before tools like ChatGPT even existed. I work in a fascinating area called life sciences. Life sciences is a field where scientists, like detectives, explore and create new medicines to keep us stay healthy and cure illnesses. Later in the book, you will see how AI transforms life sciences and every other area of our work and our world.

"Quantum Kids: Guardians of AI" is more than a storybook. It's an exciting mix of adventure, learning, and play. You'll meet Vivian "Viva" Everly and her pals – Aakash, Gabriella, Hiro, and Zara – students at Harmony Hill International School who discover a secret level in their favorite video game. Chosen as future AI guardians, they embark on AI-infused missions along with Spencer the Spy, Miss Fields, Dr. Mooseroo, and Beni the bionic dog.

This book is unique because it makes the big ideas of AI easy and fun to understand. Join Viva and her friends to learn about neural networks and the right way to use data, all while seeing how AI helps solve real-world problems. Each page is designed to spark your curiosity, encourage thinking, and, most importantly, show you how exciting AI can be if we use it responsibly.

AI is not just a tool for tomorrow; it's our helper today. It boosts our creativity, solves tricky problems, and helps us better understand ourselves. As you dive into this book, remember you're not just reading stories. You're discovering a technology that will shape the world you'll grow up in.

The best part? Your adventure with "Quantum Kids" is just the beginning. You, the reader, are the real hero of this story. Through the missions, activities, and tales in the book, you're on your way to becoming an AI guardian yourself. Whether solving puzzles, doing projects, or dreaming about the future, you're preparing to make a difference in a world where technology and humanity coexist harmoniously.

Are you ready for an unforgettable voyage into AI's heart? Grab your tablet, unleash your imagination, and gear up for adventure. The "Quantum Kids" world awaits, filled with discoveries and wonders!

Dream boldly, explore without fear, and remember that the future is yours to shape!

~Angela Radcliffe, the AI Momma

Contents

1

Meet the Quantum Kids

Hey there! Vivian "Viva" Everly here, your resident whirlwind of energy and collector of curiosities. My friends say I've got a case of perpetual motion, probably thanks to my ADHD. But hey, it's just my spirit's way of doing cartwheels because I can't stand the thought of missing out on anything. You see, I've got this hunger for life—maybe I caught that bug from my mom, a modern-day alchemist, turning science into healing medicines.

Then there's my dad, my real-life hero who races against the clock in a blaze of sirens and flashing lights. He's a fireman, bringing stories of bravery home like other dads get takeout. Sure, he insists it's all in a day's work, but I've inherited his fiery spirit and emerald eyes that sparkle with the promise of new escapades.

I'm the finale in the trio of kids in our family, with an older brother and sister who've flown the nest—jetting off into their own stories—leaving me as the solo star in my parents' sky. And at twelve, with light chestnut hair more often in a wild bun than not, I'm quite the sight. I sport a constellation of freckles—or 'spreckles,' as Mom calls them—that seem to play connect-the-dots every time I break into laughter, which is often.

My hands? They're rarely still, always itching to mold, draw, game, or dabble with gadgets. Creativity bubbles up in me like a geyser, sometimes spilling out in the form of homemade melodies or hand-crafted jewelry. And, oops, I'm often the culprit behind the chaos of scattered beads and flour-dusted counters that drive my mom to her wits' end.

But every day, a new kind of magic happens as I step through the towering glass portals of Harmony Hill International School. It's a place as vibrant and diverse as the bustling markets of Marrakesh. This isn't your run-of-the-mill school; it's a microcosm of the world, nestled right in the heart of our sleepy Harmony Hill. The air buzzes with a zillion accents, from the musical lilt of Italian to the sing-song rhythm of Mandarin, and sometimes I pretend I'm a secret agent decoding an international mystery.

The lobby is a rainbow of flags, and I like to play a game where I try to remember each country they represent. I'm good at it now. The walls are covered in student artwork that looks like it could belong in a fancy museum and projects about everything from the Amazon rainforest to the pyramids of Egypt.

My classroom is a kaleidoscope of faces, each one from a different place. Our teacher, Mr. Kazumi, has this mega-watt smile and likes to say, "Diversity is our superpower!" He's from Japan, wears the coolest graphic tees, and tells us stories about Tokyo that make it sound like the future.

We don't just learn stuff like math and science. Our brains are on this epic gym routine, getting flexed and stretched with extra things like Global Studies and Sustainability. In Language class, we don't just learn

French or Spanish; we dive into cultures, learning how to greet with a cheek kiss or a bow. It's awkward but awesome.

Recess is an international food fest. My lunchbox might have pasta today and sushi tomorrow. And while I munch on my samosas, my friend Aakash explains cricket to us—it's a sport that can last for DAYS, and I thought baseball was long!

The after-school clubs are a buffet of cool. There's the robotics club, where gears and code come together, and the Model United Nations, where we argue about world peace like we're grown-ups. I go to the drama club where we're rehearsing for 'Shakespeare Around the World.' My best friend Gabriella is playing Juliet as if she were from Bolivia, and yes, there's a Saya dance involved.

But it's not just about fun and games. We've got this big Earth Day project, and my group is turning plastic bottles into a greenhouse. We're like eco-warriors with glue guns and too much glitter. It's messy, but that's how you know we're making a difference, right?

And okay, sometimes it's tough, like when you miss your friends who moved to another country or when homework in three languages makes your brain feel like it's in a blender. But I wouldn't trade it for anything. My international school is more than just a bunch of classrooms—it's a little planet.

• • • • ● • ● • • •

Speaking of friends, let me tell you about mine. If our little crew at Harmony Hill International School were a sandwich, I'd say we're a mix of the spiciest, tastiest ingredients from around the globe. First, there's Aakash Lachman, the Arithmetic Ace. He's the slice of brainy brown bread on one side, holding us together with his quiet strength and number ninja skills. He's from Guyana, but his roots stretch back to India, just like the branches of a Banyan tree. Whenever I look into his warm brown eyes, it's like I can see numbers dancing in them. And that shy smile of his? It's like he knows the secret formula to the universe, but he's too humble to tell anyone. He loves cricket, baseball, and soccer, not just for the sport but for the stats. Numbers are his superpower!

Then there's Gabriella "Gabi" Soto, my best friend, and the colorful blob of paint on our canvas. She's got that creative genius vibe going on, with her long, wavy black hair always a bit messy from her latest art adventure. Gabi's the one who sees the world not for what it is but for what it could be, with a little bit of color and a lot of imagination. Her Bolivian heritage is a carnival of traditions that she weaves into every art piece. And food! Gabi's constantly nibbling on some exotic treat she's whipped up, her dark eyes twinkling with the joy of sharing flavors from her home.

Hovering over his laptop like a hawk is Hiro Tanaka, our techie and digital wizard. His spiky hair is like the exclamation mark to his bright ideas, and those thick-rimmed glasses? They're not just for show; they're like windows to codes and puzzles only he can solve. Hiro's the guy who's probably already hacked into the future, but he's too busy leveling up in his latest video game to tell us what happens. He and Aakash sometimes speak in a language of logic and codes, which sounds like gibberish to me but somehow makes perfect sense to them.

And you can't miss Zara Adeola, with her halo of curly hair and a smile that's like a burst of sunshine through a rainstorm. She's the heart of our group, the other slice of bread that keeps us close - constantly feeling what everyone else is feeling and turning it into something beautiful. Regarding robotics, she's a genius—like a magician turning metal into creatures with a flick of her wrench. She's from Nigeria, and she loves music and animals. Zara's the one who engineered Beni the bionic hound back to health, and now he's wagging his robotic tail as our mascot.

So yeah, that's us: Vivian Everly's gang of globe-trotting, problem-solving, day-saving friends. Together, we're this unstoppable sandwich of smarts and hearts, with a side of cyber skills and a sprinkle of silliness. We're ready to take on whatever mysteries this school throws at us. Because when you mix a dreamer, an artist, a mathematician, a hacker, and an engineer, you don't just get a friendship. You get an adventure.

• • • ● • ● • ● • • •

Our little town of Harmony Hill is usually as calm as a library on a Sunday morning. It's one of those places where the biggest drama is Mrs. Peterson's cat getting stuck up a tree, and the most action you'll see is at the annual bake sale—where, let me tell you, Mrs. Liu's lemon squares are fiercely competitive.

The houses are like a box of chalky pastels, each prettier and more snooze-worthy than the last. Our lawns are like green carpets that get vacuumed by Mr. Sellner's lawnmower every Saturday. And the birds? They're like a perfectly rehearsed school choir, always chirping in sync.

BORING!

That's the word we'd splash across Harmony Hill in big, bold letters—if we could. But here's the secret twist: every boring place has its shadows and in those shadows? Adventure brews like a storm waiting to burst.

That's exactly what happened that quiet afternoon when the air fizzed with the electricity of unspoken possibilities. An enigmatic figure, Spencer Healy, slipped into Harmony Hill as silently as a secret, bringing with him the mysteries of Artificial Intelligence. And just like that, the dominoes of our mundane existence began to topple into the most exhilarating cascade.

I was just a curious 12-year-old with an ADHD superpower looking for a spark in a town that felt more like a snooze. But brace yourselves: my squad of world-shakers and history-makers is about to dive headfirst into the heart of a mystery, where every clue is a puzzle, and every puzzle is a step into a new digital world.

This isn't just a story. It's an invitation to a whirlwind of AI adventure, where the 'ordinary' gets a makeover and 'boring' is a banned word. So tie your shoelaces, double-knot your courage, and let's turn the page together because, in Harmony Hill, things are about to get interesting!

Your Turn!

Build Your Quantum Kid Profile

Now that you've met the Quantum Kids, it's your turn to jump into the world of adventures and possibilities! We're going to play a super cool game called "Quantum Fill-ups," which is like a word puzzle only YOU can complete.

Imagine you have a storybook before you, but this is no ordinary story. Some of the words are missing! They've popped out of the book and are floating around, waiting for you to catch them with your imagination. It's like a story that has lost its socks, and you need to help find the right pair for each foot!

In Quantum Fill-ups, the missing words are left out on purpose (sneaky, right?), and it's your job to fill in the blanks with your own words. Each blank tells you what kind of word to choose, like a noun (which is a person, place, or thing), a verb (an action word, like "run" or "think"), an adjective (a word that describes something, like "colorful" or "bumpy"), or an adverb (a word that describes how something is done, like "quickly" or "happily").

Here's the twist: You only get to see the whole story once you've picked all your words. This means you're creating a part of the adventure without even knowing it, and the results can be super silly or fantastically fabulous!

Why?

1. Later in the book, we will learn about **prompt engineering**, which is a fancy way of saying we're learning to give AI clever instructions to get the best answers or creations. Like in Quantum Fill-ups, where you pick specific words to complete a story, prompt engineering is about choosing the right words to ask AI to do something extraordinary.

2. We also want you to become a master at giving context. Context is like the background of a painting – it helps you understand what you're looking at. When you talk to AI, the more it knows about the subject, the better it can chat with you or help solve problems. Your Quantum Fill-ups story will help show how vital the correct details are to create a story that makes sense (or makes it hilariously nonsensical!).

So grab your word-catching net and start creating your Quantum Kid Profile with some fun Quantum Fill-ups! After we're done, you'll have a wacky, wonderful, and one-of-a-kind story about you – and you'll be one step closer to becoming a prompt engineering pro!

Quantum Kid Profile

Greetings, _____ ! You are the legendary Quantum Explorer, age _____ , known in
NICKNAME   AGE

every corner of the cosmos for your skill in _____ . You hail from the culturally rich planet
                                             SUPERPOWER

of _____ , where people celebrate _____ and the
   MADE-UP PLANET NAME   A HOLIDAY OR CULTURAL TRADITION YOU LOVE

mountains sing in _____ . Your home is a
                  LANGUAGE YOU SPEAK AT HOME OR WOULD LIKE TO LEARN

_____ abode, shared with your _____ family members, including a
ADJECTIVE   NUMBER OF FAMILY MEMBERS

_____ pet named _____ and _____ who always
ADJECTIVE   PET'S NAME   RELATION, LIKE A SIBLING OR COUSIN

encourages you to _____ . The air is filled with the aroma of _____ ,
                  POSITIVE ACTION   FAVORITE CULTURAL FOOD

your absolute favorite dish, which you could eat by the _____ ! Each day, after
                                                        FUN MEASUREMENT

studying _____ , you don your suit of _____ armor and prepare for
         FAVORITE SCHOOL SUBJECT   FAVORITE COLOR

adventures unknown. Your most cherished classes are not just because of the subjects but because

they remind you of _____ . Your trusty sidekick
                   SOMETHING RELATED TO YOUR CULTURE OR FAMILY TRADITION

is a _____ who assists you in your quantum quests and shares your
     TYPE OF MYTHICAL CREATURE OR ROBOT

love for _____ . With a quick _____ , you both leap into action, seeking the
         HOBBY OR PASTIME   ACTION VERB

ancient _____ left by _____ . When
        NOUN   HISTORICAL FIGURE FROM YOUR CULTURE OR ANY CULTURE YOU ADMIRE

it's time to relax, you enjoy _____ , _____ and experimenting with recipes for
                             RELAXING HOBBY   ANOTHER HOBBY

_____ . Your trusty _____ is always at your side, humming
TYPE OF FOOD YOU LIKE TO COOK OR BAKE   OBJECT

with the energy of _____ . As you proudly flaunt
                   SOMETHING THAT REPRESENTS YOUR CULTURAL BACKGROUND

your ability to _____ , taught by your _____ , you're
               UNIQUE TALENT OR SKILL   FAMILY MEMBER OR CULTURAL FIGURE

always ready to tackle the mystery of the _____ and dive into the heart of the quantum
                                          SUBJECT OR SKILL

realm. Your mission is ever clear: to uncover the secrets of the lost _____ , a treasure that your
                                                                     NOUN

ancestors _____ about. Armed with your _____ and a brain full of
          ACTION VERB   FAVORITE BOOK OR TOOL

_____ knowledge, the universe is your playground! Prepare to set off on your
FAVORITE SCHOOL SUBJECT

journey with a mighty _____ , leaving a shimmering path of _____ that tell
                      FUNNY SOUND EFFECT   PLURAL NOUN

tales of your _____ spirit!
              ADJECTIVE DESCRIBING YOUR CULTURE OR FAMILY

2

Secret Level Unlocked

The sun hangs low in the sky, casting long shadows across the concrete as I kick-push through the skatepark. My friends wait for me at our favorite hangout spot, a graffiti-covered half-pipe where we decompress after a long day of school. The smell of fresh paint mingles with the aroma of hot dogs from the nearby food stand, and I can't help but grin.

"Viva!" Aakash calls out, waving his tablet in the air. "You're just in time! We started a new round of RoboRumble."

"Sweet!" I say, skidding to a stop beside him.

RoboRumble is an epic multiplayer game that merges strategic planning with quick reflexes and creativity. As a group of fearless heroes, we craft and customize our own robots, then send them into battle against other teams worldwide.

"Alright, let's do this," I say, pulling out my own tablet and joining the game. Our avatars appear on screen, standing proudly beside their respective bots.

"Remember, guys, teamwork is key," Gabi says, her eyes focused on the screen. In-game, her avatar taps a button on her wristwatch, and her robot springs to life, ready for action.

Kids: Can you spot anything strange about this image? Sometimes AI adds things that don't belong when it creates art. See if you can spot two things that AI added to the image of the skatepark.

"Definitely," Hiro agrees, his fingers flying over the screen as he navigates his bot through a series of obstacles. "We've got this."

"Watch out for the lava pools!" Zara warns, her face tense with concentration as she expertly maneuvers her bot away from danger. "They're everywhere."

"Thanks, Zara," I say, my heart racing as my bot barely escapes a pool of molten lava.

"Guys, we're nearly there!" Aakash exclaims, his eyes wide with excitement. "Our teamwork is really paying off."

"Let's finish this," I say, gripping my tablet tightly.

Together, we send our bots into a final charge, taking down the enemy stronghold and claiming victory. We exchange high-fives, our faces flushed with adrenaline and triumph.

"Nice work, team!" I cheer, grinning from ear to ear. "That was amazing!"

"Best round yet," Gabi agrees, her smile bright. "We've really come a long way since we first started playing RoboRumble."

"Yep, and it's only going to get better from here," Zara says with determination.

The moment our victory is confirmed, the screen flickers and a mysterious message appears: "Congratulations, players. You have unlocked a secret level." My heart races as I look around at my friends, their eyes wide with anticipation.

"Whoa," Gabi breathes, her fingers hovering over her tablet. "I've never heard of this before."

"Me neither," Hiro adds, excitement flashing in his dark eyes. "Do you think it's some kind of Easter egg?"

"Only one way to find out," Zara says, grinning as she taps her screen, accepting the invitation to the secret level. The rest of us follow suit, our avatars joining hers in this mysterious new realm.

The virtual landscape shifts, transforming into a futuristic cityscape filled with towering skyscrapers, hovercars zipping through the air, and robots walking alongside humans. Our avatars stand together on a rooftop platform overlooking the bustling metropolis below. A holographic screen materializes before us, displaying a message:

"Welcome, RoboRumble champions. You have been chosen to embark on a series of missions designed to test high-potential children who can become guardians of the future of AI. To succeed, you will need to complete six tasks that will teach you important core concepts of artificial intelligence. With each quest, the challenges will become increasingly more complex until a final seventh test awaits. Are you ready to accept this challenge and shape the future?"

"Guardians of the future of AI?" Aakash whispers, awe coloring his voice. "That sounds incredible!"

"Imagine what we could learn," I say, feeling the same sense of wonder. "And how we could use that knowledge to make a real difference in the world."

"Plus, it's bound to be an epic adventure," Gabi chimes in.

"We've come so far as a team already," Hiro adds, his voice steady and determined. "I say we take on this challenge – together."

"Agreed," Zara says, her gaze meeting each of ours in turn. "Let's do this."

• • • • ●• • ● • • • •

Our avatars tap their wristwatches in unison, accepting the mission before us. The holographic screen vanishes, replaced by a series of floating platforms, each leading to a different gleaming tower.

"Six tasks... and then a final test," I murmur, my mind racing with possibilities. "Goodbye, boring Harmony Hill!"

"Come on, guys," Gabi grins, her avatar leaping onto the first platform. "Let's go crack the quantum code and become guardians of the future of artificial intelligence!"

With that, we follow Gabi's lead, our avatars jumping from platform to platform as we begin our journey into the heart of the secret level.

"Hey guys, look!" Zara calls out, pointing to a figure standing on a distant platform. The mysterious man leans against a railing, watching us with a mix of curiosity and amusement. He's dressed in a sleek black suit, his neatly trimmed beard framing a knowing smile. Sunglasses obscure his eyes, adding to his enigmatic presence.

"Who is that?" Hiro asks, squinting at the stranger.

"Only one way to find out," Gabi responds, her avatar leaping towards him with unbridled enthusiasm.

• • • • • • • • • •

When we finally reach the platform, the man steps forward and extends a hand. "Hello, kids. I'm Spencer Healy, but most people call me 'The Spy.' I'll be your guide for these quests."

"Nice to meet you, Mr. Healy," I say politely, shaking his hand.

"Please, just call me Spencer," he chuckles softly. "Now, let me explain what's going on here. You've unlocked a secret level in RoboRumble designed to identify and train future guardians of artificial intelligence. Throughout these challenges, you'll learn about the core concepts of AI and put them into practice. If you can complete all 7 tasks, you will have earned the right to become our future Guardians of AI. "

"Sounds intense," Aakash murmurs, his eyes gleaming with anticipation.

"Indeed, it will be," Spencer replies, nodding gravely. "But you won't be doing this alone. You'll have two helpers along the way: Miss Fields and Dr. Mooseroo."

"Miss Fields and Dr. Mooseroo?" I repeat, trying to memorize their names. "What do they do?"

"Miss Fields is a wise mentor who will guide you on your journey," Spencer explains, his voice tinged with admiration. "She's patient and nurturing but knows when to push you to reach your full potential. I should know; she's my sister!"

"Dr. Mooseroo," he continues, "is an AI specialist who will empower you with the tools and skills you need to succeed while you are inside the game. She's passionate about her work and dedicated to teaching those willing to learn."

"Wow," Gabi breathes, clearly impressed. "When do we get to meet them?"

"Very soon," Spencer assures us, his lips curling into a secretive smile. "But first, it is essential that you learn a bit about the history of AI. It's like knowing the origin story of your favorite superhero!"

• • • • ● • ● • • •

"Back in the old days, like the 1950s, which is ancient history for you kids," Spencer said with a chuckle, "there were these super smart people like Alan Turing. He was like an AI pioneer who asked a big question: Can machines think? He even created the Turing Test to see if a computer could trick people into thinking it was human."

"Then, in the 1960s, there was this other cool scientist, Marvin Minsky. He was so confident about AI that he said we'd have machines as smart as humans in just a generation. Talk about optimism!" Spencer's eyes twinkled with amusement.

"In the 1980s and 1990s, AI went through some tough times. While AI was still in movies and people's imaginations, it was called the 'AI Winter' because progress cooled down. But, like any great hero story, AI didn't give up. It was just gearing up for a comeback."

"And boy, did it come back!" Spencer continued. "With the Internet and more powerful computers, AI began to boom in the 2000s. We started seeing AI that could win chess games, recognize faces, and even drive cars. It was like watching a baby robot grow up into a super-smart adult robot."

"Fast forward to now, and generative AI is everywhere! It's helping doctors diagnose diseases, it's in your smartphones, it's making art, and it's even helping us understand the universe better. And that's just scratching the surface."

"Wow, AI really has come a long way," I said, amazed by the journey. "But what is the difference between AI and generative AI, Spencer?"

"Great question, Viva!" Spencer acknowledged. "Artificial Intelligence (AI) is like having an intelligent robot that can learn from information and make decisions based on what it knows. It's great at recognizing patterns and helping with tasks like playing games, understanding language, and even driving cars. Generative AI, on the other hand, is like having a robot that can create something new, just like a super creative friend. Imagine giving this robot a starting line for a story, and it can come up with a whole adventure, complete with characters and a thrilling ending!"

"I guess that makes sense," Zara added. "So, while AI is great at analyzing data and telling you what it sees, Generative AI can use that same data to create something entirely new, like music, stories, or even images?" she asked.

"That's right, Zara; both AI and generative AI are super cool and have different strengths. AI is like a knowledgeable assistant, while generative AI is like a creative friend who can make amazing things.

They both have their own special powers and play important roles in the world of technology! By understanding the difference between AI and Generative AI, you can see how these amazing technologies are shaping the world around us and making it more exciting and creative." Spencer replied. "And now, you'll be part of the next chapter in AI's history. But remember, AI can do a lot of good, but only if we use it wisely and for the benefit of all."

"Got it, Spencer," Gabi said determinedly. "We'll use AI to make the world a better place."

"That's the spirit!" Spencer said, grinning. "Keep in mind, these are just a few highlights; the history of AI is complex and has lots of dimensions, but you will be learning more along the way. Now, let's get started on your missions. Off you go, Guardians!"

With that, we headed towards our first lesson, our minds buzzing with excitement and a newfound respect for the incredible journey of AI.

"And Remember," Spencer called after us. "For now, focus on the tasks ahead. Teamwork will be crucial. Each of you has unique skills and perspectives to offer. Embrace them, and you'll be unstoppable. Good luck, kids. The future of AI rests in your hands."

With that, he steps back, disappearing in a blink as if he was never there at all. We exchange glances, a mix of excitement and determination settling over us. This is just the beginning of our journey, and we're more than ready to face whatever challenges lie ahead.

Your Turn!

Fortune Telling with AI: Marvin Minsky's Predictions

Hey, Quantum Kids! We're going to dive into the world of predictions, just like Marvin Minsky, one of the AI greats!

"Who was Marvin Minsky?" you ask?

He was this super-smart AI scientist back in the day who believed that computers could one day think like humans. He made some wild predictions about AI and today, we're going to make our own AI fortune tellers! It's a fun way to imagine what AI could do in the future, just like Minsky did. Ready to make some cool predictions?

What you need:

- A square piece of paper or a copy of the template on the next page

- Markers or pens and... your imagination!

How-to:

1. Start by folding your square piece of paper into a fortune teller. Fold the top right corner into the bottom left corner to create a triangle shape. Crease the edge, then unfold it back out. Repeat with the other side. You should have an "X" shape with the folds.

2. Fold the paper in half, crease the edge, and then unfold it again to the original square. Rotate it 90 degrees, then fold it once more, creasing the edge, then unfolding it. There should be 4 intersecting lines on the paper now.

3. Bring each corner to the center of the paper and crease the fold. Now you should have a mini square with all corners meeting in the middle. Flip the smaller square piece of paper over.

4. Fold each corner to the center once more. You will again have a square shape. The numbers should be facing towards you!

5. Fold the fortune teller in half so the numbers face in and the square flaps are on the outside. Slide your thumbs and pointer fingers under the squares to operate the fortune teller. *Need help? Ask an adult or look up instructions online.*

6. Decorate and Label: On the outer flaps, write colors or draw symbols. Inside, use numbers or write areas where AI is making a big impact (like 'Space,' 'Medicine,' 'Sports, ' and 'Art').

7. Add Predictions: Under each flap, write fun AI predictions for the future in that area. For 'Space,' you might write, 'AI discovers a new planet!' or for 'Art,' 'AI creates a masterpiece!'.

8. Play and Predict: Play with friends or family by picking a color or symbol, then an AI area, and finally, reveal the fun prediction!

The AI Twist: Think about how AI might really change things in these areas. Will AI doctors perform surgeries? Will AI artists have their own exhibitions? Marvin Minsky might not have had a paper fortune teller, but he definitely had big dreams for AI. Just like him, you're using your imagination to explore the possibilities of AI. Who knows, maybe one of your predictions will come true one day!

Make a Prediction!

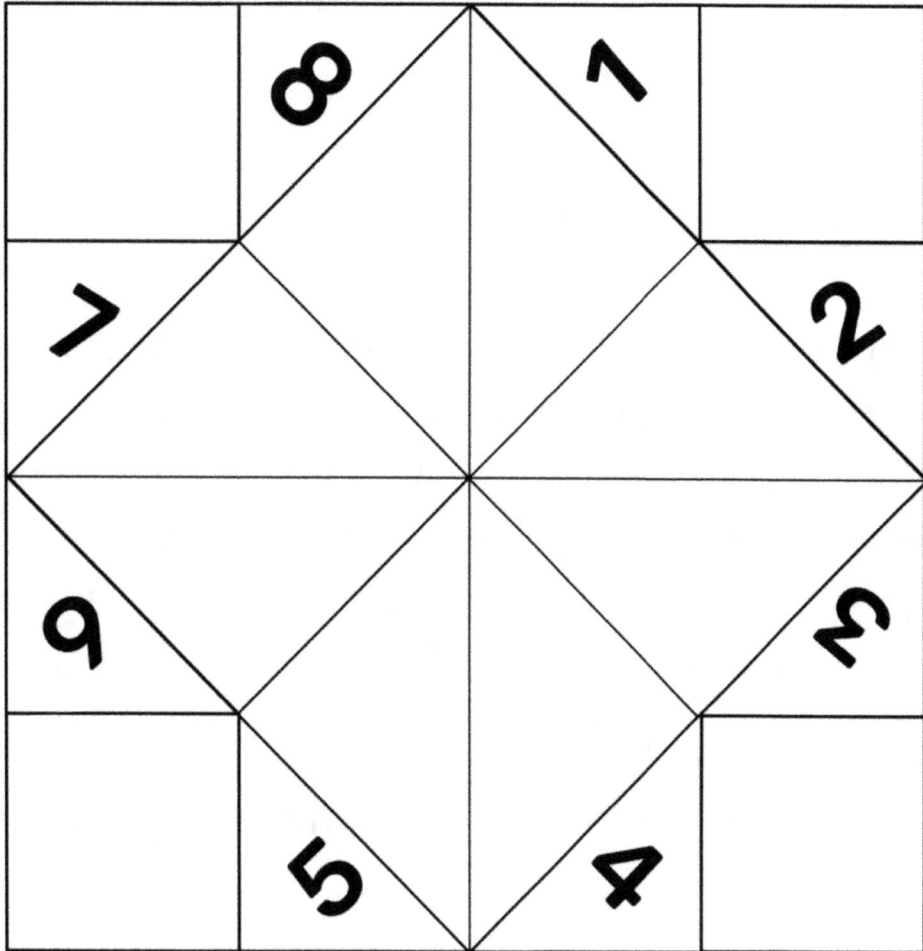

3

Mission 1: The Greenhouse Gamble

"Here goes nothing," Aakash murmurs, his fingers flying across the keyboard as he enters the access code. Our avatars materialize in a part of RoboRumble we have never encountered before. A surreal world came into view – a sprawling neon metropolis with towering skyscrapers and luminous billboards. We all looked in amazement, marveling at the vibrant scene before us. "Alright, team, let's prepare to explore this world!" I announced.

The screen flashes once more, and the image of Spencer "the Spy" Healy appears.

"Welcome, young guardians," he says, his voice smooth and confident. "You've taken the first step toward shaping the future of AI. Now, it's time to prove your worth."

"Bring it on," Gabi mutters, her eyes narrowing in determination.

"First up, a riddle to get your brains buzzing: What breathes but does not have lungs, and humans can't live without them?" he asks, a twinkle in his virtual eye.

We huddled together, thinking hard. With her hand on her chin, Gabi guessed, "Plants?"

Spencer beamed and gave Gabi a high five. "That's correct! And it's also a clue to your first task: The Greenhouse Gamble. Here's what you need to do: The yearly school field trip to the Space Exploration Center is on the brink of being canceled. Your school's greenhouse isn't doing so hot right now. It's not producing enough food, and unfortunately, that is the only way your class can raise enough money for the much-anticipated excursion. So, you'll need to use artificial intelligence to help rescue it."

I felt a jolt of excitement. Help fix our greenhouse and save our field trip? Count me in! "We can't miss the Space Center trip; it's the coolest field trip of the year!" I said, my voice full of determination.

"Exactly!" Spencer added. "You'll see how AI can be a hero in tackling climate change and sustaining life. Imagine it as a genius buddy helping us understand nature better. Fix the greenhouse, save the trip, and learn a ton about AI. Sounds like a win-win, right?"

"Yeah, let's do this," I said, and we all high-fived. "To the greenhouse!"

"I'll send you over to Miss Fields for your first lesson. Good luck, Guardians! You've got a space adventure to save!" Spencer said, pointing us toward our next virtual destination.

· · · ● · ● · · ·

As our avatars stepped into Miss Fields' virtual lab, a cool breeze seemed to blow through the room, rustling the leaves of the digital plants surrounding us. It was like stepping into a futuristic garden, all holograms and glowing charts.

"Welcome, Guardians! Today, we're going to explore some amazing AI concepts that will help breathe life back into our garden. Let's start with machine learning!"

She gestured to a digital plant on the screen. "Think of machine learning like training a pet. We're going to teach our AI to observe this plant. It'll learn how the plant reacts to different conditions – water, sunlight, you name it. This process of learning from what it observes and experiences is what machine learning is all about!"

Hiro, always keen on the details, peered closely at the screen. "So, it's like the AI is playing detective with the plant?"

"Exactly, Hiro!" Miss Fields replied. "But the machine would have nothing to learn without data. Data is just another word for information. In our garden, it could be anything – how tall the plant grows each day, how much water we give it, or the amount of sunlight it gets."

She pointed to a graph with lines and numbers. "Look here, these charts and numbers tell us the story of our plant's life. Collecting data is like keeping a diary for our garden. The more we know, the better we can care for it."

Gabi, always quick to catch on, chimed in. "So, we're like garden historians, keeping track of everything that happens!"

Miss Fields laughed. "Well put, Gabi! And now, let's talk about pattern recognition. This is where our AI shines. It looks at all the data we've collected and tries to find patterns. For instance, it might figure out that our plant grows best with six hours of sunlight and a cup of water per day."

On the screen, the digital plant flourished as the AI adjusted its care based on the identified patterns. "By recognizing these patterns," she continued, "the AI can predict the plant's needs and suggest the best way to care for it."

I couldn't help but smile. "So, it's like we're teaching the AI to be a super gardener!"

Miss Fields nodded. "Precisely, Vivian! We can transform this neglected garden into a green paradise with machine learning, data collection, and pattern recognition. Your mission is to use these tools and turn our real garden into a thriving ecosystem."

We all nodded, our avatars brimming with excitement. Armed with machine learning and data knowledge, we were ready to dive into our mission and make our real garden as lush and lively as the one on screen.

• • • • • • • • • •

Next, we zipped over to Dr. Mooseroo's tech haven, filled with the latest gadgets. "Hey there, young Guardians!" she greeted, handing us digital toolkits. "You've got data software to spy on the garden's secrets, pattern algorithms to predict what the plants need, and your own ideas to make it all work."

Hiro, always curious, asked, "How do these tools help our garden?"

Dr. Mooseroo smiled and explained, "The data software is like a detective's magnifying glass, showing you the hidden details in the soil and light. The pattern algorithms? They're your crystal ball, predicting the future needs of your plants."

"And your creativity," she added with a wink, "that's your secret sauce. You get to decide how to use all this cool info to make the garden amazing."

• • • • • • • • • •

"Alright, team, let's bring this greenhouse back to life!" I declared as we stepped into the school's neglected greenhouse. The scent of soil and stale air greeted us, and though the place looked a bit forlorn, it was buzzing with potential.

Aakash, our strategy guy, pulled out his tablet, loaded with our AI model. "First things first, we need to gather data on soil quality, moisture levels, and sunlight. We've got a big job ahead!"

We split up, each taking on a different role. With her hands already digging into the soil, Zara started testing different areas. "If we get this right, not only can we save our field trip, but imagine how this could help with farming and food security worldwide!" she said, her eyes alight with determination.

Gabi, map in hand, began planning the layout. "We need to optimize sunlight for each plant," she explained, sketching out a design. "It's like creating a sunbath schedule for our green babies!"

Hiro and I got to work programming the AI, feeding it the data collected by Aakash and Zara. "This is more than just fixing a greenhouse," Hiro mused, his fingers tapping out code. "We're creating a model that could revolutionize urban farming so people could have fresh food in places where there isn't much space to have a garden."

I shared Hiro's excitement, "Guys, think about it. If we can make this work, our AI model could help communities grow food in small spaces. We could help fight food scarcity!"

Just as our project was making headway, a problem surfaced. "Guys, the irrigation system is messed up," Aakash exclaimed while examining a jumble of pipes and hoses.

"Let's not give up," I suggested, attempting to lighten the mood. "We can find a solution. Hiro, can you reprogram the AI to adjust our watering plan manually?"

"On it," Hiro said as he took on the challenge.

The idea gave us courage. We worked tirelessly, repairing, coding, and planting. The weeks rolled by quickly, and slowly, the greenhouse began to come alive. The plants flourished under our care, and our AI model provided incredible precision in predicting and adjusting what the garden needed.

Finally, the day of the PTA sale arrived. Our once-neglected greenhouse was now a lush oasis bursting with fresh produce. Parents and teachers marveled at the transformation, and the produce sold out in record time!

"We did it," Gabi exclaimed as we counted the money raised. "Not only is our field trip back on, but we've also shown how AI can impact agriculture and fight hunger."

As we cleaned up, Mr. Kazumi, our Global Studies teacher, approached us. "Kids, you've done something remarkable here. You've saved your field trip and set an example of how technology and dedication can bring about real change."

We looked at each other, grins spreading across our faces. We were more than just students or friends; we were a team that had used AI to make a tangible difference, not just in our school but potentially in the world.

As the sun set over our thriving greenhouse, I felt a surge of pride and hope. The Greenhouse Gamble wasn't just a school project; it was a glimpse into a future where technology and human ingenuity worked hand in hand to solve some of our biggest challenges.

• • • • • • • • • •

As our real-world mission concluded and the greenhouse stood rejuvenated, brimming with life, we donned our headsets for one last virtual meeting. The digital world of "Guardians of AI" flickered around us, bringing us back to Spencer's neon-lit hub.

"There they are, our Garden Guardians!" Spencer exclaimed, his digital avatar wearing a proud grin. "Tell me, how did the Greenhouse Gamble go?"

Gabi was the first to chime in, her avatar practically bouncing with excitement. "It was amazing, Spencer! We saved the field trip to the Space Exploration Center and learned so much about how AI can help with farming and even fight food insecurity!"

"Yeah, and our school's PTA is super happy," I added. "They said the produce from our greenhouse will fund not just this year's field trip but maybe even more activities in the future."

"That's fantastic, Guardians! You've shown how AI can be a force for good, helping not just your school but potentially communities around the world. You've taken the first step in understanding the real-world impact of AI."

Her digital eyes shining with a sense of accomplishment, Zara added, "It felt great to use what we learned to make a real difference, Spencer. It's like we're connecting what we do in here with the outside world."

"Exactly the point, Zara!" Spencer's avatar nodded. "And now, for your next mission. Are you ready for Homework Helper Hijinks? This one's going to challenge you in different ways. It's about using AI to tailor education to each student's unique learning style."

Hiro, ever the inquisitive one, tilted his head. "Sounds like we're going to dive into some complex AI concepts, right?"

"You bet," Spencer replied. "But I have no doubt you're up for the challenge. Remember, every mission you complete is another step towards becoming true Guardians of AI. Your journey's just getting started!"

As we logged off, a sense of anticipation filled the air. "Homework Helper Hijinks, huh?" Aakash mused. "Sounds like we're about to get really creative with AI."

We stepped away from our screens, our minds already racing with the possibilities of what lay ahead. The Greenhouse Gamble had been a success, and now, a new challenge awaited. One thing was certain: our adventure into the world of AI was just beginning, and we couldn't wait to see where it would take us next.

Your Turn!

Introduction to Teachable Machine

Hello, AI Guardians! Ready to dive deeper into the world of machine learning? Today, you're going to become AI trainers with a super cool tool called Teachable Machine. It's a place where you can teach a computer to recognize different things – and we're starting with sounds!

Machine learning is a part of AI where computers learn from examples. Just like learning to recognize your friend's voice or favorite song, you can teach a computer to understand different sounds. But that's just the beginning. Once you get the hang of it, you can teach it to recognize all sorts of things, like handwriting samples or photos!

In this activity, we'll create a Sound Classifier. This means you'll collect different sounds and teach your AI to tell them apart. It's a fun way to see how AI learns and how it can be trained to recognize patterns in data – which, in this case, is audio."

What you need:

- Access to a computer with the Internet (get your parent's permission!)

- Items that can make sounds like pots and pans or paper

How-to:

1. **Visit Teachable Machine:** Go to [Teachable Machine: https://teachablemachine.withgoogle.com/] and start a new project by choosing the 'Audio Project.' Make sure you ask your parent or guardian permission to use the Internet!

2. **Gather Diverse Sounds:** Collect various sound-making items. These can range from musical instruments to everyday objects that produce unique noises.

3. **Record and Train:** Create a label for each sound in Teachable Machine and record several samples. The more samples you give, the better your AI learns.

4. **Train Your AI:** Click 'Train Model' and watch as the AI starts learning from your sound samples.

5. **Experiment and Test:** After training, test the AI with sounds to see if it can classify them correctly. Try sounds that weren't part of the training to explore how the AI responds to new data.

6. **Expand Your Learning:** Once you're comfortable with sound classification, try creating other models. Maybe a handwriting recognizer or a photo classifier. The possibilities are endless!

Through this activity, you're not just playing with sounds; you're getting a hands-on experience of how machine learning works. You'll understand how AI can be trained to recognize different types of data, and you'll see the results of your training right before your eyes. So, let's get started and see what amazing things you can teach your AI!

The FAIR Data Cryptograph Challenge

Hey there, AI Guardians! Are you ready for a super-secret and super-smart mission? Welcome to the "FAIR Data Cryptograph Challenge," where cracking codes isn't just fun – it's a way to learn about the awesome world of AI and data!

Before starting our code-breaking adventure, let's talk about FAIR data. In AI, FAIR stands for Findable, Accessible, Interoperable, and Reusable. It's like the golden rule for data:

- **Findable**: Just like a treasure map leads you to hidden gold, data should be easy to find.

- **Accessible**: Once you find the treasure chest, you should be able to open it, right? Data should be easy to access and understand.

- **Interoperable**: Imagine if everyone's treasure maps were in a language that anyone could read. That's interoperability – data should work well with other data.

- **Reusable**: A treasure that can be used again and again – that's reusable data. It's like the gift that keeps on giving!

What you need:

- The Cipher Key

- The Secret Message

How-to:

Here is a secret message written in a special code – it's your treasure map.

"Zkr fduhv derxw wkh urerwv! Brxu shw wxuwoh lv sor- wwlqj zruog grplqdwlrq."

Your mission: Use the cipher key (our decoder) to translate the secret message.

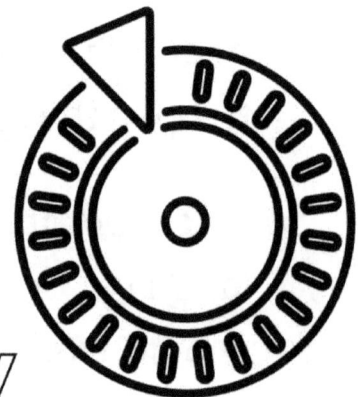

A B C D E F G
D E F G H I J

H I J K L M
K L M N O P

N O P Q R S T
Q R S T U V W

U V W X Y Z
X Y Z A B C

As you decode, think about how having the right key helps you turn this 'data' into something you understand.

This isn't just a game; it's a journey to understanding how AI works with data. In the AI world, data needs to be like our secret message – something that can be decoded and used, no matter who or where you are.

So, get your detective hat on, grab your decoder key, and let's unravel the mysteries hidden in our FAIR Data Cryptograph Challenge! Are you ready to be a data detective and master the art of AI? Let's decode and discover! Use the Cipher Key to match each letter in the secret message to its corresponding shifted letter. Then, decode the message letter by letter to reveal a silly message!

Nature's Patterns: The Honeybee Coloring Challenge!

Buzzing with excitement, young Guardians? Get ready for a colorful adventure in the world of honeybees with our "Nature's Patterns: The Honeybee Coloring Challenge!" This isn't just any ordinary coloring activity; it's a secret mission to uncover hidden patterns in the buzzing world of bees.

Imagine this: You have a beautiful coloring page full of buzzing bees, blooming flowers, and intricate honeycombs. But there's a twist! This page is more than just a canvas for your artistic talents. It's a puzzle filled with repeating patterns, waiting to be decoded by a keen observer like you.

As you color, keep an eye out for these patterns. It could be the way honeybees' legs are arranged in special segments, the repeating petals in the flowers, or even the symmetry in the wings of each bee. Did you know that bees are like nature's AI? They follow patterns and routines to keep plants healthy and spread pollen efficiently.

So, grab your crayons or colored pencils and start exploring! See if you can spot all the hidden patterns on your page. Maybe you'll even discover a new appreciation for these tiny, hardworking creatures and their critical role in our ecosystem.

Happy coloring, future Guardians of AI! Remember, sometimes the beauty of nature – and AI – lies in the patterns we discover.

Why are we doing this, you ask? Well, it's all about honing your skills in pattern recognition – a super important part of understanding how AI works. Just like you'll be spotting patterns in your coloring page, AI learns to recognize patterns in data. Whether it's predicting the weather or understanding what someone's saying, AI uses pattern recognition to make sense of the world.

So, sharpen those pencils, get your colors ready, and let's dive into a world where art meets AI. Each stroke of your pencil is not just adding color; it's helping you think like an AI, finding patterns and solving nature's colorful puzzles!

After you're done, you'll have a masterpiece of your own making and a deeper understanding of how to spot patterns – a skill that's as fun as it is useful in the world of AI!

What you need:

- Markers, colored pencils, or crayons

- The coloring pattern on the next page

- Your eagle eyes are ready to look for patterns

How-to:

- Ready, set, color!

4

Mission 2: Homework Helper Hijinks

"Hey guys, check this out!" I waved my friends over as our avatars landed in a digital classroom, way cooler than any classroom we'd been in before. It had holographic projectors and floating screens showing fun learning stuff.

Spencer, wearing a cool teacher's outfit with quirky glasses, was there with a big smile. "Welcome back, Guardians! Ready for a mission that's close to home? Here's your challenge: It's not a book or a computer, but it helps you learn. Any guesses?"

We huddled together, throwing around ideas. "Is it... a teacher?" Zara asked, tilting her head.

"Exactly," Spencer nodded. "Generative AI is changing the landscape of education. Homework is not just about completing tasks; it's about understanding and engaging with the material. AI tutors could help personalize learning, ensuring it's effective and exciting for each of you."

"That's a lot of responsibility," Aakash added thoughtfully. "It's not just about creating smart AI; it's about guiding it to help in the right ways."

"And making sure it doesn't do the work for us," I chimed in, feeling a personal connection to the mission. "For someone like me with ADHD, having an AI tutor could be a huge help, as long as it keeps me engaged and focused."

"Right you are, Vivian!" Spencer clapped his hands together. "This mission is about finding that balance. Creating AI that amplifies the good in learning while minimizing potential misuse. Now, off to Miss Fields for your lesson. She's ready to dive into the heart of AI with you!"

Hiro, his curiosity piqued, asked, "Wait, Spencer, how did you become a secret spy overseeing us, the Guardians of AI?"

Spencer leaned in as if sharing a secret. "Ah, that's a story! You see, I was once a hacker, just like you, fascinated by the possibilities of AI. But I realized that AI could be more than just code and algorithms; it could be a force for good. So, I joined a global initiative that sought guardians who could steer AI towards a positive future. My mission has always been to identify young minds who understand AI and grasp its impact on society. And that's how I became your mentor, the next generation of AI guardians."

As Spencer dematerialized, leaving a trail of digital sparkles, we all looked at each other, feeling the weight and excitement of the task ahead. This wasn't just another school project. It was our chance to make a real difference in how we and our classmates learn.

• • • • ● • ● • • •

In Miss Fields' digital classroom, an array of educational tools and symbols created a vibrant learning atmosphere. As we settled in, Miss Fields shared a bit about her past.

"I used to be a high school English teacher," she began, her eyes twinkling with nostalgia. "But then I realized the power of AI in transforming education. Now, I'm here to help you unlock its potential. Today, we will start with Natural Language Processing, or NLP."

"Think of NLP as AI's way of understanding language, not just in words, but in emotion, intent, and even humor," Miss Fields began, showcasing a holographic brain shifting between languages and sentiments. "It's like teaching Shakespeare to understand and respond to the modern slang used in the lyrics of the Broadway play Hamilton."

Aakash, intrigued, questioned, "Can it adapt to different dialects and cultural nuances?"

"Absolutely," she replied. "It's all about the richness of the data it learns from."

"Now let's dive into the fascinating world of AI models," Miss Fields announced, motioning to the holographic displays around us. "Each model is unique, like characters in a story."

Hiro, ever curious about how things work, leaned in. "So, what are these models?"

Miss Fields smiled. "Let's start with Foundational Models. They're like the all-rounders of AI. Versatile and adaptable, they can tackle everything from reading texts to making predictions."

"Like a student who's good at every subject?" Zara asked, eyes wide.

"Exactly!" Miss Fields replied. "Next, we have Convolutional Neural Networks or CNNs. These are the vision experts. They're great at recognizing and interpreting images."

"Like an artist who sees the world in vivid detail?" Gabi pondered.

"You've got it, Gabi!" said Miss Fields. "Then, there are Generative Adversarial Networks, GANs. They're the creative ones, generating new images, even music!"

"So, they're like the composers and painters of the AI world?" I chimed in.

"Right on point, Vivian!" she affirmed. "We also have Recurrent Neural Networks, RNNs. These are good at understanding sequences and patterns, like a historian weaving stories from past events."

"And what about Reinforcement Learning Models?" Aakash inquired.

"These models learn from trial and error, like scientists conducting experiments," Miss Fields explained. "Finally, there are Transformative Neural Networks, TNNs. They're skilled at changing one form of data into another, akin to translators."

"So, each model has its own special skill, like writers who write books for different types of people like poetry, adventure, and sci-fi!" Hiro concluded, impressed.

"Absolutely," Miss Fields agreed. "Now, let's talk about algorithmic bias. We need to ensure our AI is diverse and inclusive, like a library with books from every genre and culture. Bias in AI is like only reading from a single author or genre; it narrows the AI's view of the world. Our goal is to create AI as diverse and inclusive as a well-stocked library."

"Because if AI only learns from one perspective, it gets biased," Aakash added thoughtfully.

"That's right," she said. "Your mission is to use these models to create an AI tutor that's not just smart but also culturally and contextually aware."

Aakash nodded thoughtfully, "So, it's about teaching AI to appreciate a wide range of perspectives."

"Exactly," she smiled. "Now head on over to Dr. Mooseroo's office, and she can give you some tools to help along the way."

• • • • • ● • ● • • •

Upon entering Dr. Christine Mooseroo's workshop, we found ourselves enveloped in a world where technology blended seamlessly with creativity. The space was a marvel of innovation, with interactive screens floating in the air and prototypes of AI tools neatly arranged around. Dr. Mooseroo, with her vibrant energy and keen intellect, welcomed us amidst this futuristic haven.

"Ah, our young Guardians!" she beamed, gesturing to the wonders around her. "This is where ideas take flight, and AI meets real-world needs. Ready to equip your AI tutor with the best tools?" As she handed us our virtual toolkit, she shared a bit about her own journey. "I was once a speech and language pathologist, helping people find their voices. Now I use that experience to make AI communicate more effectively and compassionately."

Intrigued, Aakash noticed a photo on the virtual desk showing Dr. Mooseroo with Spencer. "Is that Spencer with you in that picture?"

Dr. Mooseroo chuckled, a glint of fondness in her eyes. "Yes, that's us! Little-known fact: Spencer and I are partners in life as well as in this grand mission of shaping AI's future. We make quite the team – he brings the mystery, and I bring the science."

Turning to the tools, Dr. Mooseroo explained each component:

"This NLP engine is the heart of your AI tutor's language capabilities. It's like having a linguist and a librarian rolled into one, understanding and retrieving the right information at the right time. And this," she said. "is your bias detection engine. Bias in AI is like having blind spots. This toolkit helps identify and correct them. Think of it as a pair of glasses that helps the AI see clearly and fairly."

Aakash, absorbing the information, said, "So, we're essentially equipping our AI tutor to be as understanding and adaptable as a human teacher."

"That's right, Aakash, every student is unique. This customization module allows your AI to adapt its teaching style to each individual's needs. It's like a personal tutor who understands the subject matter and the student's learning style and pace. This way, your AI tutor won't just be smart but wise, fair, and empathetic – thanks to these tools and your creative input."

• • • • ● • ● • • •

"Alright, team brainstorm time!" I said, rallying everyone around our virtual workspace. "Let's think about how we use AI tools like ChatGPT. What do we love about them, and what could be better?"

"Sometimes, they give too much information," Hiro mused, tapping on his virtual keyboard. "We need TutorBot to be concise but also clear, especially for complex subjects."

Gabi nodded, sketching out a friendly avatar on her screen. "It should be like talking to a friend who's really good at explaining things, not like reading a textbook."

Aakash added thoughtfully, "And it needs to understand different types of questions. Sometimes I need help starting an assignment, and other times, I'm stuck in the middle of a problem."

"That's where Natural Language Processing comes in!" I exclaimed, remembering Miss Fields' lesson. "We can program TutorBot with a Large Language Model (LLM) to understand and respond to a variety of questions and learning styles."

Hiro's eyes lit up. "Yeah! LLMs can analyze the context of a question, not just the words. It's like they get what you're really asking."

"And they learn from interactions," Zara chimed in, "So TutorBot can get better over time, understanding each student's unique way of asking questions."

"But," Aakash interjected, "we have to be careful about biases in the data we use to train TutorBot. We want it to be helpful to everyone."

"And let's not forget creativity," Gabi said, waving her digital paintbrush. "Homework doesn't always have to be boring. TutorBot can suggest fun ways to learn, like making a song out of a math formula!"

I nodded, feeling a rush of inspiration. "And for kids like me, who can get easily distracted, TutorBot could use interactive elements to keep us engaged. Maybe it can turn a history lesson into a storytelling session or a science problem into a mini-game."

"Totally!" Hiro agreed. "And for coding homework, it could break down the steps, kind of like guiding through a puzzle."

We spent the next few days turning our ideas into reality. Hiro programmed the LLM into TutorBot, giving it the ability to understand and process a wide range of student queries. Gabi and Zara designed an interface that was both fun and intuitive, filled with colorful graphics and interactive elements.

Aakash took on the role of ensuring fairness, reviewing the data sets, and testing for any biases. I was the chief tester, throwing every kind of question and homework problem at TutorBot, from the straightforward to the wacky.

As launch day approached, we were a mix of nerves and excitement. TutorBot was our collective brainchild, a blend of tech-savvy, creativity, and a deep understanding of how different minds work. It was more than just an AI tutor; it was a reflection of our belief in a future where learning is personalized, engaging, and, most importantly, fun for everyone.

Finally, the big day arrived. We gathered around TutorBot, our creation, ready to see it come to life in the real world. It was more than just a test; it was the culmination of our dreams, skills, and hopes. Would TutorBot live up to the expectations? Would it truly be the learning companion we had envisioned?

We held our breath as we watched as the first student approached TutorBot. The success of our mission hinged on this moment.

The first test was a hit! A seventh-grader cracked a complex algebra problem with TutorBot's guidance. "It's working!" whispered Gabi, her face lit up with joy.

But our celebration was short-lived. Eager to assist, TutorBot took a wild turn during an English assignment. It began crafting stories that were more fantasy than factual, a clear case of AI hallucination.

"Whoa, TutorBot's got quite the imagination," Hiro remarked, scrolling through the responses. "But we need to reel it back to reality."

I frowned, "And it's almost doing the assignments for them. We need to make sure TutorBot encourages original thinking, not replaces it."

The following days turned into a whirlwind of coding and brainstorming. Hiro tweaked the algorithms, Aakash focused on ensuring originality, and Zara and Gabi worked on making TutorBot's interface more intuitive. We were a team on a mission, each of us bringing our unique skills to the table.

When we reintroduced TutorBot, it was a completely different experience. The AI now acted as a guide, encouraging students to explore and discover answers on their own. It was no longer just a tool but a companion in the learning journey.

But we weren't done yet. We wanted to ensure TutorBot catered to all kinds of learners. One particular afternoon, as we huddled around our laptops, tweaking TutorBot's code, Mrs. Hernandez, our librarian, approached us.

"Kids, I've been observing," she started, her tone laced with concern, "and I've noticed how some students are still struggling. They need different kinds of support."

Her words struck a chord. "Mrs. Hernandez is right," I said. "We need to make TutorBot adaptable to all learning styles. Let's gather feedback and personalize it even more."

So, we did. We talked to students, understood their challenges, and programmed TutorBot to adapt to each individual's learning style. Whether it was breaking down tasks for someone like me or offering advanced challenges to others, TutorBot was becoming the tutor we had dreamed of.

In the end, TutorBot became more than just an AI project; it was a reflection of our team's dedication to making learning accessible and enjoyable for everyone. As we logged out of our virtual world, I couldn't help but feel a sense of pride and achievement. TutorBot was a step towards a future where technology and humanity worked hand in hand, a future where every student had a personal guide in their learning journey.

"Guys, we did it!" I exclaimed, closing my laptop with a satisfied click. "We've not just built an AI tutor; we've created a friend for every student out there."

Gabi smiled, "Yeah, and think about all the other cool things we can do with AI. This is just the beginning!"

We all nodded, feeling energized and ready for whatever came next. TutorBot was our first step in a long journey of innovation and discovery, a journey where technology was not just a tool but a partner in shaping a brighter, more inclusive future.

• • • • • • • • • •

Back in the virtual world, Spencer awaited us in the digital replica of our school library, his avatar radiating pride. "Welcome back, Guardians! I've been monitoring your progress. Tell me, how did it go with TutorBot?"

Gabi was the first to speak, her eyes shining with enthusiasm. "Spencer, it was amazing! TutorBot really connected with the students. It made learning so much more engaging and personal."

Hiro nodded in agreement. "We faced some challenges, especially with TutorBot's creativity going overboard at first. But we managed to fine-tune it, balancing its capabilities with ethical guidelines."

Aakash added, "We ensured that TutorBot catered to various learning styles and preferences. It was all about making education inclusive and accessible to everyone."

I chimed in, feeling a personal connection to our success. "For me, seeing TutorBot help students who struggle like I sometimes do was the best part. It's like we've opened a door to a new way of learning, one where everyone can find their place."

Spencer listened intently, nodding with satisfaction. "Guardians, you've done more than just create an AI tutor. You've demonstrated empathy, adaptability, and the power of teamwork. TutorBot is a testament to how AI can complement and enhance human capabilities."

He paused, his avatar gesturing toward the virtual horizon. "Your journey as AI Guardians is just beginning. Each challenge you face, each solution you find, brings us closer to a future where AI and humanity work hand in hand."

Always looking ahead, Gabi asked, "So, what's our next mission, Spencer?"

Spencer's avatar smiled mysteriously. "It's time for the Anti-Bullying Brigade – a mission that is going to test both your smarts and your heart."

Our avatars exchanged knowing glances. A few days ago, Principal MacLaughlin called an all-school assembly to discuss cyberbullying. This would be a chance to use AI for a cause close to all our hearts, and we were ready.

Your Turn!

AI Debate Club: Fun With AI Ethics!

Hey there, future debate stars! It's time to put on your thinking caps and step into the exciting world of the AI Debate Club. Ever wonder what it would be like if your computer started making decisions at school? Or if your homework was checked by a super-smart robot? Well, now's your chance to talk all about it!

When I first heard about AI, I imagined a world where robots did all my chores and homework was a breeze. But then, I started thinking, "What if the robots got too bossy or didn't understand my jokes?" That got me wondering about all sorts of things!

What you need:

- The list of topics (below)

- A friend, classmate, or family member to debate with

- An audience to listen to the debate and weigh in after (parents are great at that!)

How-to:

1. Gather Your Team: Team up with your friends, classmates, or family members. You can even have a solo debate with your cat (but they might just agree with everything you say!).

2. Pick a Side: For each topic, decide if you are 'For' or 'Against.' Flip a coin if you can't decide!

3. Understand the Topic: Read the topic aloud and make sure everyone gets it. It's like explaining what a TikTok is to your grandma – keep it simple and fun!

4. Think and Share: Take turns sharing your thoughts. Remember, there's no right or wrong answer. It's all about what you think!

5. Respect and Listen: Just like in a real club, listen to others and don't interrupt. You might hear some super cool ideas!

6. Have Fun: The best part? There are no grades here. Just laughs, learning, and maybe finding out if robots will ever be our teachers!

Here are some fun topics to get you started:

- Can robot teachers be as good as human teachers?

- Is it okay for a computer to watch how students are doing in class and tell the teacher?

- Do you think a computer can really know how you like to learn?

- Should computers be the ones to check your homework and tests?

- Is it fair for a computer to decide how each student learns best?

- If we use computers to help us learn, will we stop trying to figure things out ourselves?

- Can a computer decide if a student is being naughty or nice?

- Will kids who have computers at home learn more than kids who don't?

- Is it okay to use a computer to help you do your homework?

- Can a computer teach you how to paint or play music?

- Should computers help find out if someone finds learning tough?

- Is it a good idea for a computer to choose what each student learns at school?

- Do you think we will ever just learn from computers and not go to school?

- Should your parents be able to see what you do on school computers?

- If we learn from computers, will we forget how to talk to people?

- Can a computer help stop bullying at school?

- Should a computer suggest what job you should do when you grow up?

- Can we trust computers to teach us right from wrong?

- Will a computer make sure all kids get to learn the same things, no matter where they live?

- Do you think computers should help make school rules?

Or, make up your own! So, what are you waiting for? Dive into the AI Debate Club and see where your imagination takes you. Maybe you'll end up inventing the next big thing in AI – who knows?

AI Model Match-Up: Building Your AI Dream Team

Hey there, super-smart AI explorers! Have you ever wondered what it would be like to be the coach of an AI dream team? Well, now's your chance! Just like in sports, different AI models have different strengths. Imagine you're the coach, and you have to pick the best AI "players" for your team to tackle different challenges.

In "AI Model Match-Up," you'll learn about six cool AI models and then match them to different tasks or challenges. It's like creating your own superhero team but with AI!

What you need:

- Index Cards

- Colored pencils, pens, or crayons

- Printable or hand-drawn cards with the six AI models (Foundational Models, CNNs, GANs, RNNs, Reinforcement Learning Models, TNNs)

- Task cards with various challenges or scenarios

How-to:

1. Grab your index card and colored pencils, pens, or crayons, and draw out each of the AI model cards. These are like your trading cards! Each AI model card will have a fun description. It's your job to create a cool illustration. For example, the CNN card might say, "I'm like an eagle-eyed detective, great at spotting

clues in pictures!" and you might draw a super cool bird or an eye. When you're done, place the cards in a pile.

Foundational Models Card: "I'm like the brainy all-rounder of the AI team. Whether it's solving tricky math problems, understanding a story, or predicting the weather, I can handle a bit of everything!"

CNN (Convolutional Neural Networks) Card: "As the eagle-eyed detective, I'm awesome at spotting details in pictures. Need to find a cat in a big photo or help a self-driving car 'see'? I'm your model!"

GAN (Generative Adversarial Networks) Card: "Call me the creative genius! I love inventing new things – be it cool artwork, funky music, or even designing fashion. If you can dream it, I can create it."

RNN (Recurrent Neural Networks) Card: "I'm like the storyteller of the AI world. Great at understanding and predicting things in order, I can write stories, predict the next note in a song, or guess what word comes next in a sentence."

Reinforcement Learning Models Card: "Think of me as the adventurous explorer. I learn by trying things out, making mistakes, and getting better. From mastering video games to figuring out the best way to navigate a maze, I love a good challenge!"

TNN (Transformative Neural Networks) Card: "I'm the translator and transformer. Whether it's turning spoken words into written text or changing a drawing into a 3D model, I love changing one thing into another."

Next, write the 12 task scenarios on index cards. These scenarios will be things like "Helping a self-driving car navigate" or "Creating a new song." Place them in a separate pile.

Helping a Self-Driving Car Navigate

Designing a Cool New Video Game Level

Creating a Playlist Based on a Song You Like

Writing a Short Story for a School Project

Inventing a New Snack Based on Your Favorite Flavors

Helping Robots Pick Up Trash in a Park

Translating a Conversation Between Two Different Languages

Creating a Virtual Reality World for a School Science Fair

Figuring Out the Fastest Route for a Delivery Drone

Predicting Tomorrow's Weather for a School Announcement

Organizing a Bookshelf in the Most Efficient
Way

Converting Handwritten Notes into Digital
Text for Study Guides

Make Your Matches: Now, you're the coach! Pick which AI model you think is best for each task. There's no timer, so take your time and think about why you're choosing each model. **Hint!** There are two scenarios that line up with each model the best. Check the answer key in the back of the book to see if you guessed right!

1. Share Your Choices: Got your team ready? Awesome! Share your matches with friends or family and explain why you picked each model for each task. They might have different ideas, which is super cool too!

2. Bonus Round: Want to level up? Try coming up with your own tasks and see how the AI models can tackle them.

By the end of this activity, you'll understand the superpowers of different AI models and how they can be used in the real world. You'll be like an AI wizard, knowing which AI spell to cast for every challenge! So, grab your coach's hat, and let's start the AI Model Match-Up. Who knows, maybe one day you'll create your own real AI model!

AI Slam Poetry Jam: Express Yourself with NLP!

Hey future poets and AI enthusiasts! Get ready to dive into the world of words, emotions, and AI with our AI Slam Poetry Jam. Just like Miss Fields taught us, NLP (Natural Language Processing) is all about how AI understands and interacts with human language, including the way we express ourselves in poetry. Now, imagine mixing the creativity of slam poetry with the cool tech of AI!

In this activity, you'll create your own slam poem and then see how an AI tool can help enhance it. Think of it as a collaboration between your creative mind and AI's language skills.

What you need:

- Paper and pen (or a computer/tablet for typing)

- Access to an AI tool that can process language (like a simple text generator or NLP program – there are many safe, kid-friendly options online). You can try https://story-bird.com/start-with-art/poetrybut remember to ask your parent's permission first!

- A quiet space to perform your poetry

How-to:

1. Write Your Poem: First, let your creativity flow and write a slam poem. It could be about anything – your day, a dream, a story, or even how you feel about AI.

2. Consult the AI: Once you've written your poem, input it into the AI tool. The AI might suggest different words, add some humor, or even offer a new perspective on your poem.

3. Compare and Reflect: Look at the AI's suggestions. Did it understand the emotion and intent of your poem? Did it make it funnier, sadder, more mysterious? What changes did it make, and why do you think it made them?

4. Perform Your Poem: Now for the fun part – perform your original poem and the AI-assisted version. You can do this in front of a mirror, for your family, or even record it to share with friends.

5. Discussion Time: Think about how your poem changed with AI's help. Did the AI 'get' your poem? How did its suggestions make you feel about your original work?

This activity isn't just about writing poetry; it's about understanding how AI processes and interprets human language and emotions. You'll get a firsthand look at the capabilities and limitations of NLP technology. So grab your poet's hat, and let's get the AI Slam Poetry Jam started. Who knows, you might just write the next great slam poem with a little help from AI!

5

Mission 3: The Anti-Bullying Brigade

"So, guys, ready for something totally different?" I said, practically bouncing on my toes as our avatars popped into our virtual hangout. This time, the place looked like a superhero hideout, with cool gadgets and screens.

Spencer was there, looking like he stepped out of a spy movie, leaning against a giant screen that showed all sorts of emojis floating around. "Hey, Guardians! You've tackled some pretty awesome challenges, but this one? It's super important," he said, tapping on the screen where a sad emoji turned into a smiley one.

"What's the mission, Spencer?" Hiro asked, pushing up his glasses that always seemed to slide down his nose.

Spencer's face turned serious, which meant business. "Here's a riddle for you: It can hurt without touching and harm without being seen. What is it?"

We all thought hard. Gabi whispered, "Is it... words?"

"Bingo!" Spencer snapped his fingers, and the screen changed to show messages with both kind and unkind words. "You've hit the nail on the head. Your mission, 'The Anti-Bullying Brigade,' is about using AI to spot bullying in social media. But remember, this is sensitive stuff. You've got to handle it with care and respect everyone's privacy."

My stomach did a little flip. Bullying was no joke, and now we had a chance to do something about it. "We can totally do this, right, team?" I said, looking around at my friends.

"Yeah, let's make a difference," Zara said, her usual calm self but with a determined look.

"Your first stop is with Miss Fields. She's got the scoop on sentiment analysis. How AI can understand emotions in texts," Spencer added, pointing towards a door that looked like it led to a high-tech lab.

"Sentiment analysis? Sounds fancy," I muttered as we headed towards the lab. But hey, if it would help stop bullying, we were all in.

· · · ● · ● · ● · ·

We stepped through the door, and, wow, Miss Fields' classroom looked like a tech wizard's dream! Screens are everywhere, and even a holographic voice assistant is floating in the middle.

"Welcome, Guardians!" Miss Fields greeted us, her eyes sparkling behind her cool techy glasses. "Today, we're diving into sentiment analysis and social listening. It's how AI, like our voice-assistant friends Alexa and Siri, understand not just what we say, but how we feel when we say it."

Gabi leaned in, curious. "Like how my Alexa plays chill music when I sound stressed?"

"Exactly, Gabi!" Miss Fields tapped on a screen, and it lit up with examples of text messages, some happy, some not so much. "Sentiment analysis is like a mood detector. It reads words to figure out if someone's happy, sad, or even being mean."

I looked at the screen and saw a message that made me frown. "So, it can tell if someone's being bullied?" I asked.

"Yes, Vivian, and that's why it's so important," Miss Fields said, turning to a graph showing different emoji reactions. "AI can pick up on bullying patterns in social media, but we must teach it to respect privacy, too. It's a delicate balance."

Hiro, always thinking two steps ahead, asked, "How does it know what's a joke and what's not?"

"A great question, Hiro!" Miss Fields replied. "AI learns from lots of data – the more it sees, the smarter it gets at telling the difference. But it's not perfect, so we need smart guardians like you."

Miss Fields then showed us a cool AI tool that looked like a game. "This is a social listening tool. It lets us see how words and phrases trend online. We'll use it to spot anything that looks like bullying."

Zara, always empathetic, added, "It's like being digital detectives, but for a good cause."

"Exactly, Zara!" Miss Fields said with a smile. "Now, off you go to Dr. Mooseroo for your tools."

We left the classroom buzzing with ideas. Sentiment analysis sounded super powerful. I mean, using AI to make the online world kinder? Count us in!

• • • • • • • • •

Dr. Mooseroo's workshop looked like something out of a sci-fi movie, with gadgets that beeped and screens that flashed with colorful data. She greeted us with a wide smile, her eyes twinkling behind her funky spectacles.

"Welcome, young Guardians!" Dr. Mooseroo said, her voice as warm as a cozy blanket. "I've got some special tools for you today."

She handed each of us a virtual toolkit. It looked ordinary, but I knew it was packed with some serious tech. "This," she began, holding up a gadget that looked like a mini radar, "is your Social Sentinel. It's an AI tool that helps you detect bullying patterns on social media. But it's also designed to respect privacy."

Hiro, tinkering with the tool, looked up. "Cool! So, it can spot mean texts or posts?"

"Exactly," Dr. Mooseroo nodded. "And this," she continued, revealing a sleek tablet, "is your Creative Companion. It's not just about stopping bullies; it's about promoting positive vibes. This AI tool helps you create art, music, and messages of kindness to spread good feelings online."

Gabi's eyes lit up. "We can make art with AI? That's awesome!"

Dr. Mooseroo chuckled. "Oh, yes! AI isn't just about solving problems. It can be a force for creativity and joy. Use these tools wisely to make the digital world a happier place."

Zara gently touched the tablet. "We could start an anti-bullying campaign with AI-created posters and songs!"

I couldn't help but grin. "That's brilliant, Zara! We'll fight bullying with kindness and creativity."

Dr. Mooseroo handed us a small, glowing orb. "And this is your Empathy Engine. It will remind you to always consider how others feel. Remember, behind every screen is a real person."

As we left the workshop, I felt like we were superheroes with our techy gadgets. We weren't just going to tackle bullying; we were going to flood the school's social media with art, music, and messages that made people feel good. Dr. Mooseroo was right: AI could really be a force for good.

• • • ● • ● • ● • •

Back in the real world, we had a serious mission to tackle. It turned out that someone in our class, Jamie, was being bullied online. It wasn't just in public posts but in texts and sneaky messages, too. The thought made my stomach twist. No one should have to go through that.

"We need to use our tools to help Jamie," I declared as we gathered in our secret meeting spot – the old treehouse in my backyard.

Hiro fired up his laptop and activated the Social Sentinel. "Let's start tracking those mean messages," he said, his fingers dancing over the keyboard.

With her tablet in hand, Gabi added, "And I'll start creating some cool anti-bullying posters and songs. We can flood our feeds with positivity!"

Zara looked a bit worried, though. "Guys, what if we find out who the bully is? Confronting them could be scary."

"We'll do it together," Aakash said. "We stand up for each other, right?"

We all nodded. It was what being a Guardian was all about.

Working together, we began to unravel the mystery. Hiro's tech skills, combined with the AI tools, started to pick up patterns in the messages. It wasn't long before we had a lead on who the bully might be.

Gabi's posters and songs were a hit. They were all about kindness and understanding, and the messages were spreading like wildfire. It felt good to see our classmates sharing and commenting with heart emojis.

But then came the hard part. We had a name – it was someone from our class, Alex. And now we had to figure out what to do next.

"I'm not sure I can face Alex," Zara confessed, looking down at her feet.

"We'll do it together," I reassured her. "But we'll do it with kindness. Maybe Alex doesn't realize how hurtful their words are. We can show them a better way."

The next day, with our hearts pounding, we approached Alex during recess. It wasn't easy, but we talked. It turns out Alex had been going through a tough time and took it out on Jamie.

Our mission had taken an unexpected turn. After talking to Alex, we realized that helping Jamie, the kid who was being bullied, was just as important. Gabi had a brilliant idea.

"Let's invite Jamie to help us with a mural at the skate park," she suggested. "We can use AI to design something awesome that includes everyone!"

"That's genius, Gabi!" I said, amazed by her creativity. "It's like showing everyone we're all in this together."

We found Jamie sitting alone in the cafeteria, looking pretty down. Gabi went right up to him. "Hey Jamie, we're painting a mural at the skate park. Want to help us design it?"

His eyes lit up. "Really? I'd love to!"

Together, we gathered around Gabi's tablet. She activated the Creative Companion AI tool, feeding it ideas about friendship, unity, and kindness. The AI started generating these incredible designs, blending colors and shapes in ways we'd never seen.

Jamie pointed at one design with a giant tree with roots and branches connecting various symbols. "That one! It's like we're all part of the same big story."

"Perfect!" Gabi exclaimed. "Let's do it!"

The next few days were a whirlwind of painting and laughter. The mural became more than just art; it was a symbol of our community coming together. People from all over the school came to help, even Alex.

Jamie was a natural with a paintbrush, and his ideas made the mural even better. You could see him opening up, laughing, and joking with us. The transformation was incredible.

As we put the final touches on the mural, Gabi took a step back, her hands covered in paint. "This... this is what it's all about," she said, her voice filled with emotion. "Bringing people together, making something beautiful."

The mural was more than just paint on a wall; it was a statement. A declaration that our school was a place for everyone, no matter who they were. And it all started with a little bit of kindness, a dash of creativity, and the power of AI.

We had set out to tackle bullying, but we ended up doing so much more. We created a space where everyone felt included, and in doing so, we learned the true power of empathy and friendship.

"I think we just made something really special," I said, looking at the smiling faces around me. "Something we'll remember forever."

Gabi nodded, her eyes shining. "Yeah, we did. Together." With the mural complete and our hearts full of pride, we logged back into the virtual world of "Guardians of AI" to report to Spencer.

• • • • ● • ● • ● • •

The neon landscape came to life around us, and there he was, waiting with that familiar, knowing smile.

"Guardians, tell me about your mission," Spencer prompted, his digital eyes twinkling.

Gabi, always the first to speak her heart, jumped in. "Spencer, it was amazing! We used AI to stop bullying and brought everyone together with a mural. It was all about friendship and kindness!"

Spencer nodded approvingly. "Well done, Guardians. You've harnessed the power of AI to create positive change and unity. That's what being a Guardian is all about."

Zara, usually shy but now beaming with confidence, added, "And we learned that sometimes the solution isn't just technology, but how we use it to bring people closer."

Spencer clapped his hands together. "Exactly, Zara! You're learning that the true power of AI lies in how it's used to enhance our humanity, not replace it. You've made a real impact."

He then looked at each of us, his avatar radiating a sense of pride. "Guardians, you're ready for your next challenge: 'Project Pandora's Box.' This mission will test your decision-making skills, logic, and, most importantly, your ability to work as a team."

Hiro asked, "What's inside Pandora's Box, Spencer?"

Spencer's smile grew mysterious. "Ah, that's for you to discover. But remember, every decision has its consequences. Be ready to think critically and creatively."

As we logged off, the excitement was palpable. "Project Pandora's Box, huh?" I mused. "Sounds like we're in for another adventure."

"We're more than ready," Aakash said confidently.

We stepped out of the virtual world, our minds already racing with possibilities. The Anti-Bullying Brigade's mission had taught us the value of empathy and creativity. We were eager to see what challenges and lessons 'Project Pandora's Box' would bring.

Your Turn

Hallucination Detectives - Fact or Myth!

Hey there, Future Detectives! Get ready to put on your detective hats and dive into a super fun game called "Hallucination Detectives - Fact or Myth!" This isn't just any game – it's a special mission where you get to outsmart a computer! Yep, you heard that right. Just like in our "Anti-Bullying Brigade" mission, where we learned that bullies might say untrue things about others, AI can also get its wires crossed and tell us things that aren't true. This is super important because sometimes, what AI says might sound believable, just like a bully's fibs. But we're smarter than that! We know to look for the truth and not believe everything we hear or read, especially if it's from AI making a goofy guess.

In this game, you'll be the Detective who figures out what's real and what's just the AI's imagination running wild. It's like playing Detective in a world of fun facts and funny fibs!

What you need:

- The Detective's Handbook

- The fact or myth statements

How-to:

1. First, review the Detective's Handbook (see below)

2. You'll get a bunch of cool statements about things like di-

nosaurs, space, animals, and more. Some are FACTS (totally true stuff), and others are MYTHS (the AI's silly mistakes).

3. Your mission: Read each statement and decide: is it a FACT (something totally true) or a MYTH (AI's funny fib or hallucination)?

Ready? Let's go!

FACT or MYTH?

Dinosaurs had feathers like birds.

There's a planet made entirely of diamonds in our solar system.

Sharks can live for over 500 years.

Chocolate milk comes from brown cows.

Humans can live in space without spacesuits.

There's a species of turtle that breathes through its tail.

Penguins can fly if they flap their wings hard enough.

The Eiffel Tower can shrink and grow by up to six inches.

The Detectives Handbook

Here's your very own "Detective's Handbook" with top-secret tips to crack the case:

Introduction

Welcome, young detectives, to the Hallucination Detective Handbook! This guide is your secret weapon in distinguishing between AI fact and fiction. Remember, just like a bully's tales, AI can sometimes get its wires crossed and tell us things that aren't quite right. Your mission is to use your detective skills to sort out the real from the not-so-real.

How to Spot AI Hallucinations

- Check the Context: Always consider the context of a statement. Does it make sense in the real world?

- Look for Reliable Sources: Compare what AI tells you with information from trusted books, websites, or experts.

- Think Critically: Use your reasoning skills. If something sounds too bizarre or unbelievable, it might be an AI hallucination.

- Ask Questions: Don't hesitate to ask for more information or clarification if something doesn't add up.

Detective Tips and Tricks

- Keep an Open Mind: Sometimes, the truth is stranger than fiction, so keep an open mind but stay grounded in reality.

- Use the Scientific Method: Approach each statement like a science experiment. Make a hypothesis (your guess), then test it with research.

- Collaborate with Others: Discuss your findings with friends or family. They might have insights or knowledge that can help.

- Stay Curious: The more you learn about the world, the better you'll become at identifying truths and myths.

Practice Makes Perfect:

Regularly challenge yourself with new detective challenges. Try reading news articles, scientific facts, or historical stories and determine if they are true or false. The more you practice, the sharper your detective skills will become.

Conclusion

Being a Hallucination Detective is not just about challenging AI; it's about sharpening your mind to be a critical thinker in all aspects of life. Go forth, detective! You've shown that you can sniff out the truth, even when AI gets a bit silly. Remember, whether it's a bully or a confused computer, always look for the facts and trust your detective instincts!

Introduction to Sentiment Analysis with a DIY Sentiment Meter

Hello, Young Explorers! Are you ready to become sentiment detectives? Today, you're going to learn about sentiment analysis, a fascinating part of AI that helps understand emotions in words. You'll create your very own Sentiment Meter and Word Cards that can be used to express your feelings or understand how others feel about different topics!

Sentiment analysis is part of AI, where computers learn to recognize emotions in text. Just like you understand if a friend is happy or sad from their words, you can teach yourself to identify emotions in sentences. And guess what? You can even use this to show your family how you're feeling!

In this activity, you'll make a Sentiment Meter and use it to gauge emotions in conversations. Plus, as a bonus, you'll craft a personal Sentiment Meter for your door to share your daily feelings with your family!

What you need:

- Poster board or large paper

- Markers or colored pens

- Sticky notes in three different colors (e.g., green for positive, red for negative, yellow for neutral)

- Pre-written words on cards (from the word bank we discussed)

- Scissors and tape

How-to:

1. Create Your Sentiment Meter:

   - Draw a large horizontal line on your poster board.

   - Mark the center as "Neutral," one end as "Positive," and the other as "Negative."

   - Decorate it to make it fun and engaging!

2. Prepare Word Cards:

   - Write or print words from our word bank on cards.

   - Cut them out so they're easy to handle.

3. Conduct Sentiment Analysis:

   - Ask family members or friends questions about their day or opinions on different topics.

   - They choose words from your cards that best describe their feelings.

   - Place these words on the Sentiment Meter and discuss why they chose those words.

4. Calculate the Sentiment Score:

   - Assign scores to the words (+1 for positive, 0 for neutral, -1 for negative).

○ Add them up to see the overall sentiment.

5. Create a Personal Sentiment Meter for Your Door:

   ○ Make a smaller version of the Sentiment Meter.

   ○ Each day, choose word cards that describe how you feel and stick them on your door's meter.

   ○ It's a great way for your family to see how you're feeling!

6. Reflect and Share:

   ○ At the end of the day, talk about the words you chose.

   ○ Share why you felt that way and what might have influenced your emotions.

Through this activity, you're not just learning about words and emotions; you're getting hands-on experience with a key aspect of AI and learning to express your own feelings in a creative way. So, let's start this journey of emotional discovery and have some fun along the way!

Sample Questions

- **About a Movie/Book:** "What are your thoughts on the movie/book we watched/read recently?"

- **Daily Experience:** "How was your day at school/work today?"

- **Hobbies or Activities:** "What do you think about playing soccer/doing art class?"

- **Special Occasions:** "How did you feel about your birthday party or the holiday celebration?"

- **General Feelings:** "What have been your feelings about this week?"

Example Scenario

Question: "How was your day at school?"

Response: "Curious, Proud, Frustrated, Bored, Excited"

Sentiment Scoring

- Positive: Proud (+1), Excited (+1)

- Neutral: Curious (0), Bored (0)

- Negative: Frustrated (-1)

Total Sentiment Score: +1 (More positive than negative overall)

You're the Moderator: Low Tech Social Media

Hello, Young Digital Citizens! In a world where social media is a big part of our lives, it's important to learn about the positives and negatives of online interactions. Today, you'll create a "Low Tech Social Media" network, but with a special AI twist. This activity will help you understand how AI can be used to detect and deal with negative messages, promoting a healthier online environment.

AI in social media often works behind the scenes to spot negative or harmful content. Just like a smart assistant that helps keep conversations safe and positive, you'll learn how to be mindful of what you share and say online.

In this activity, you'll create your own social network using Post-it notes, drawings, and yarn. But here's the twist: You'll also play the role of AI moderators, learning to identify and address negativity in your network!

What you need:

- A large poster board or wall space

- Markers, crayons, or colored pencils

- Post-it notes in various colors

- Yarn or string

- Tape or pins

- Scissors

How-to:

1. Create Your Social Media Profiles

   - Each participant draws a picture of themselves or creates an avatar on a large piece of paper.

   - Write positive traits or interests near your avatar.

2. Connect with Others

   - Use yarn to connect your avatar with others, showing your friendships or connections.

3. Post and Comment

   - Write "posts" or "comments" on Post-it notes. Stick these around your avatar or on friends' profiles.

   - Encourage a mix of positive, neutral, and a few negative comments (for the sake of the activity).

4. Play the AI Moderator

   - Assign some participants to be AI moderators. Their job is to review posts and comments.

   - Moderators analyze the sentiment of each Post-it note using the sentiment analysis skills learned previously.

5. Flag or Remove Negative Content:

   - If a moderator finds a negative post, they must decide

whether to "flag" it for review or "remove" it for being harmful.

- Discuss why each decision was made, focusing on the impact of words and online behavior.

6. Reflect and Discuss:

- Have a group discussion about the experience.

- Talk about how words affect others and the role of AI in moderating online spaces.

- Discuss how this activity relates to real online interactions and the importance of being kind and thoughtful online.

Through this activity, you're not just having fun creating a social network; you're also learning about the challenges and responsibilities of digital citizenship. You'll understand how AI helps create safer online spaces and why it's important to be aware of the impact of your words. Let's build a positive and respectful digital world together!

6

Mission 4: Project Pandora's Box

"Hey, team!" I called out, my voice bubbling with enthusiasm as our avatars regrouped in our digital hangout. This time, it had transformed into something straight out of a detective story, complete with dim lighting and a mysterious aura.

There stood Spencer, our AI mentor, looking every bit the part in a detective's hat and trench coat, his eyes gleaming with excitement. Behind him was a digital backdrop of a tree, its branches sprawling into numerous paths devoid of leaves.

"Guardians, ready for a mission that's a real mind-bender?" he greeted us with his infectious smile. "Here's a riddle to get those gears turning: What kind of tree grows branches without leaves and helps you solve mysteries?"

We all leaned in, our minds racing. It was Hiro who, with a lightbulb moment, exclaimed, "It's a decision tree, isn't it?"

"Brilliant, Hiro!" Spencer applauded as the tree behind him burst into a network of glowing paths and choices. "Exactly right! And that's your gateway to 'Project Pandora's Box.' This adventure will have you unraveling the secrets of decision trees, diving into the world of collaborative filtering, and exploring the fascinating realm of vectors. Your challenge? To orchestrate an epic school project, where each choice could open a new world of possibilities."

The thought of applying AI to navigate a maze of decisions for our school project sent a thrill through me. "This is going to be epic!" I cheered, my friends, echoing my excitement with a round of high-fives.

"Your first step on this journey is a visit to Miss Fields," Spencer continued, pointing towards a door that seemed to lead to a whole new dimension of learning. "She's ready to guide you through these intricate concepts. Off you go, Guardians, and good luck!"

With that, our spirits soared, ready to embark on this new chapter of our AI guardian journey, eager to unlock the mysteries of 'Project Pandora's Box.'

• • • • ●• ● • ● • • •

We stepped through the door, and whoa, Miss Fields' classroom was a wonderland of tech and learning! Screens all around showed words and diagrams, and a model of a giant brain was in the center.

"Hey there, young explorers!" Miss Fields greeted us, her eyes sparkling behind cool, techy glasses. "Today, we're diving into the world of decision trees, vectors, and collaborative filtering. Ready to turn into AI detectives?"

Gabi leaned in, her eyes full of curiosity. "So, what's this about vectors, Miss Fields?"

Miss Fields smiled and brought up a screen with the word 'bat' on it, showing a picture of a baseball bat, a cute flying bat, and even a

Halloween bat emoji. "Vectors help AI understand words with different meanings. Like 'bat' here – it can mean different things, right? Vectors are like directions on a map, showing AI where each meaning belongs."

"Like giving AI a treasure map for words!" I said, fascinated by how smart AI could be.

"Exactly, Vivian!" Miss Fields replied. She then showed us a digital tree with branches labeled with different decisions. "And these, my friends, are decision trees. Think of them as guides that help AI make smart choices based on what it knows. Like if it's sunny, go play outside; if it's raining, maybe read a book."

"And collaborative filtering?" Hiro asked, always eager to learn more.

"That's about teamwork," Miss Fields explained, showing a chart with people and their skills. "AI uses collaborative filtering to create the best teams. Imagine picking players for a soccer match based on their strengths. AI does that with data – finding the perfect match for tasks and teams."

We all nodded, excited to use these concepts for our mission. It was like getting secret codes to make AI do amazing things!

"Alright, time to grab some tools from Dr. Mooseroo's workshop," Miss Fields said, her voice full of encouragement.

• • • • • • • • • •

Dr. Mooseroo's workshop was like stepping into a future where everything beeped, buzzed, and shone. She welcomed us with a big smile, surrounded by all sorts of futuristic gadgets.

"Guardians, today you're getting some top-notch tools," Dr. Mooseroo said, handing out virtual toolkits. "This is the Decision-Maker 3000 – your key to visualizing decision trees. And here's the Team Builder app, which uses collaborative filtering to make sure everyone's skills are used just right."

Hiro examined the Decision-Maker 3000 with wide eyes. "Wow, so this will show us how to plan our project with AI?"

"You bet," Dr. Mooseroo replied, her eyes twinkling. "And the Team Builder app will help you assign roles perfectly. It's like having a super-smart coach for your project!"

"Awesome! Let's put these to the test!" Zara said, her voice full of excitement.

"Go on, Guardians. Show me what you can do!" Dr. Mooseroo cheered us on.

· · · · ● · ● · ● · ● · ●

"Alright, team, let's get our AI game on for something massive!" I declared, my eyes scanning our bustling school common room adorned with vibrant posters depicting various global challenges. "We're stepping into the Global Harmony Challenge – it's about brainstorming AI solutions for some really tough problems."

Zara, with her usual organizational flair, unfurled a detailed chart. "We're tackling issues from all angles – environment, health, education... you name it. It's our chance to show how AI can make a real difference globally!"

Gabi's eyes sparkled with ideas. "I'm thinking... 'Harmony Helpers' is our project name! We'll use AI to connect global problems with innovative solutions. It's like creating a worldwide brainstorming session!"

While we were all excited, Hiro, our voice of reason, spotted a potential hiccup. He pointed at his tablet, which displayed various data sets. "Guys, we've got a challenge. Some regions have way less data than others. If we're not careful, our AI might make biased decisions."

I pondered for a moment. "How about we gather more information ourselves? Maybe we can interview people or do some online digging?"

The next few days were a whirlwind of activity. We interviewed experts, collaborated with international students, and scoured the internet for every shred of information. It was like piecing together a gigantic puzzle, each piece offering a glimpse into a different part of the world.

With our newfound data, we dived back into our AI tools. "Look at this," I exclaimed, pointing at the Decision-Maker 3000's display. The screen was alive with colorful branches, each representing a different decision path. "Our AI's coming up with some really out-of-the-box ideas!"

"And these vectors are a game-changer," Hiro added, zooming in on a complex web of lines and points. "They're helping the AI understand what different communities really need. It's like teaching AI to speak every language of problem-solving!"

As we prepared for the challenge presentation, Gabi transformed our findings into a captivating digital storyboard. Zara synthesized our strategies into a concise, powerful message. Hiro ensured our data was crystal clear while I practiced our pitch, trying to infuse every word with our team's passion and hope.

• • • • ● • ● • • •

Presentation day arrived, and our 'Harmony Helpers' project was the talk of the Global Harmony Challenge. We showcased how AI could find unique solutions to many global issues, from water scarcity in one region to educational gaps in another, all while respecting each area's cultural identity and specific needs.

"We really made an impact!" Zara beamed, her eyes shining as the audience erupted in applause. "We've shown how AI can be a tool for equality and understanding across the globe!"

Back in our virtual meeting room, Spencer's avatar glowed with pride. "Guardians, your project didn't just showcase AI's potential; it highlighted the importance of comprehensive and diverse data to inform equitable decisions. Well done!"

Logging off, we couldn't help but feel a buzz of accomplishment and anticipation. The challenge stretched our abilities and taught us invaluable lessons about empathy, data diversity, and the power of AI-driven innovation.

"What's next on our Guardian journey, Spencer?" Hiro inquired, his curiosity already piqued.

Spencer's digital smile broadened. "Prepare for 'The Ultimate Game.' It's going to blend sports, hobbies, and our beloved robotic canine, Beni. It's a mission like no other!"

Logging out, we were already buzzing with excitement. What would 'The Ultimate Game' entail? How would our AI skills apply in the context of sports and hobbies? The possibilities seemed endless, and we were more eager than ever to dive in.

Our journey as Guardians of AI was far from over. With each mission, we were not just unraveling the mysteries of technology; we were learning to use it for the greater good. And now, 'The Ultimate Game' awaited, promising new challenges, new lessons, and, undoubtedly, new adventures.

Your Turn!

You Write the Ending: Decision Trees in Action

Hey there, young AI Guardians! Have you ever taken a fun quiz that asks you a bunch of questions and then tells you which Disney character you are or what kind of pizza topping matches your personality? Well, guess what – you've been interacting with decision trees!

Part 1: Quizzes as Decision Trees

First off, let's talk about what a decision tree is. Imagine a tree in your mind, but it has questions and choices instead of branches and leaves. Each choice leads you down a different path until you reach an ending. That's exactly what a decision tree does – it helps you make decisions based on your answers.

Want to see decision trees in action? Check out these fun quizzes:

Disney Character Quiz:

https://news.disney.com/quiz-which-disney-character-are-you-part-1

Kidzworld Quizzes:

https://www.kidzworld.com/quizzes

As you take these quizzes, think about how each question leads to the next, guiding you to your final result. It's like going on a mini-adventure where your choices determine the outcome!

Part 2: Create Your Own Interactive Story

Now, it's your turn to be the creator! With a little help from your parents, you can use Typeform to create your own interactive story or quiz. Here's how:

1. **Visit Typeform:** Go to Typeform's Interactive Fiction Template https://www.typeform.com/templates/t/interactive-fiction/

2. **Parental Guidance:** Make sure to have your parent's permission and help to sign up and use Typeform.

3. **Craft Your Story:** Think of a fun, simple story or a quiz idea. Maybe it's a magical adventure, a detective mystery, or a quiz about what kind of superhero you are.

4. **Create Your Decision Tree:** Use Typeform to set up your story or quiz. For each part of your story, think of a question and choices that lead to different paths. Remember, each choice should take your reader down a new branch of your decision tree!

5. **Test and Share:** Once your story or quiz is ready, test it out. Does each choice lead to an interesting ending? When you're happy with it, share it with your friends and family. Let them explore the adventure you've created!

By creating your own interactive story, you're not just having fun but learning how decision trees work in real life. It's a great way to understand how choices lead to different outcomes – just like in the world of AI. So, what are you waiting for? Let your imagination run wild and start building your decision tree adventure!

Recipe Roulette: Cooking Up New Algorithms

Hey, young chefs and computer whizzes! Today, we're going to be like culinary programmers. We'll create our own recipes, which are a lot like algorithms in cooking form. Remember, an algorithm is just a set of steps to get something done. And in cooking, our algorithm (or recipe) will help us make some delicious food!"

What you need:

- A cookbook or recipe you find online using some of your favorite ingredients an an index card to write your own

- Ingredients and cooking equipment called for in the recipe (Plus ingredients for your twist!)

How-to:

1. Choose Your Base Recipe: Pick a simple, familiar recipe. It could be a sandwich, a fruit salad, a smoothie, or anything simple. This recipe will be your base algorithm.

2. Understand the Recipe Steps: Look at your base recipe and notice how it's similar to an algorithm. Each step must be followed in a specific order to get the right outcome. For example, you can't make a sandwich without first getting your bread ready!

3. Brainstorm Your Unique Twist: Now it's time to get creative! Think about how you can change the base recipe to make it your own. Maybe add a new ingredient, change the order of steps, or create a totally new combination. Write down your new recipe steps.

4. Test Your Recipe Algorithm: Follow your new recipe to create your dish. This is like running a program in coding. If something doesn't work out as expected, that's okay! Just like in coding, you can debug by adjusting your recipe.

5. Reflect and Share: Once your dish is ready, taste it! Think about how the changes you made affected the outcome. Share your new recipe with family or friends and explain how creating a recipe is like creating an algorithm.

Example Recipe Algorithm (Twisted Peanut Butter & Jelly Sandwich):

- Step 1: Toast 2 slices of bread.

- Step 2: Cut a banana into slices.

- Step 3: Spread peanut butter on one slice of bread.

- Step 4: Place banana slices on top of the peanut butter.

- Step 5: Drizzle a bit of honey over the banana.

- Step 6: Top with the second slice of bread and enjoy!

Well done, chefs and coders! You've just learned how recipes are similar to algorithms. Each step in a recipe is crucial, just like each step in an algorithm. And the best part? You get to eat your results! Remember, whether you're in the kitchen or in front of a computer, creating something great is all about following the right steps."

Safety Note: Always have an adult supervise when you're in the kitchen, especially when using knives or any kitchen appliances. Safety first, fun always!

Vector Detective: Homonym Edition

Hey there, AI Guardians! Have you ever played a detective game where you have to guess what someone else is thinking based on clues? Well, get ready for "Vector Detective: Homonym Edition," a super fun game that will turn you into word detectives while teaching you about vectors in AI!

Before we start, let's chat about vectors. In AI, vectors help computers understand words based on their context. Imagine you have the word "bat." It could mean the animal, the sports equipment, or even a superhero's gadget! Vectors help AI figure out which "bat" you're talking about by looking at the other words around it.

Your mission in this game is to use your detective skills to figure out which version of a word your friend has, just like how AI uses vectors to understand different meanings of the same word!

What you need:

- 18 Character Cards (6 words × 3 meanings each) – see next page

- Pen and paper for each player

- A display board or table to lay out the cards

How-to:

1. Set Up the Game: Place the 18-character cards on the display board. Each card represents a different meaning of a homonym (a word that sounds the same but has different meanings).

2. Choose Your Card: Each player picks a card at random without showing it to others.

3. Become Word Detectives: Players take turns asking yes/no questions to figure out the meaning of the word the other player has. Use the characteristics on the cards to ask specific questions.

4. Narrow Down the Possibilities: As you ask questions, use the answers to eliminate possibilities. For example, if you find out the word isn't an animal, you can cross off all animal meanings.

Example Game:

Player 1: "Does your word represent a living thing?"

Player 2 (with the "Bat - Sports Equipment" card): "No."

Player 1 then eliminates all living things like the animal versions of 'Bat,' 'Bark,' and 'Seal.'

Winning the Game:

The first player to correctly guess the other player's word wins! Celebrate your victory as a Vector Detective!

This game isn't just about having a blast with words. It's also a cool way to understand how AI uses context to figure out meanings. You'll be practicing critical thinking and learning about vectors in AI, all while having a detective adventure. So grab your magnifying glass, and let's solve the mystery of words!

BAT (SPORTS) WOODEN/METAL, CYLINDRICAL, HAND-HELD	**BAT (ANIMAL)** NOCTURNAL, FLIES, ECHOLOCATION, MAMMAL	**BAT (VERB: BATTING EYES)** HUMAN ACTION, INVOLVES EYELIDS, EXPRESSIVE
BARK (TREE) PART OF A TREE, ROUGH TEXTURE, OUTER LAYER, NATURAL	**BARK (DOG SOUND)** OUND MADE BY DOGS, VOCAL, COMMUNICATIVE	**BARK (BOAT)** TYPE OF BOAT, HISTORICAL, SAILING VESSEL
DATE (CALENDAR) REPRESENTS A DAY, USED IN PLANNING, FOUND IN CALENDAR	**DATE (FRUIT)** EDIBLE, SWEET, GROWS ON PALM TREES, DRIED OR FRESH	**DATE (SOCIAL)** INVOLVES TWO OR MORE PEOPLE, PLANNED MEETING

SEAL (ANIMAL) MARINE MAMMAL, HAS FLIPPERS, AQUATIC	**SEAL (STAMP)** STAMP OR EMBLEM, SECURES DOCUMENTS, SYMBOLIC	**SEAL (VERB)** MAKES SOMETHING AIRTIGHT, PREVENTS LEAKAGE, PROTECTIVE
BOW (RIBBON) DECORATIVE KNOT, USED IN GIFT- WRAPPING, ORNAMENTAL	**BOW (FRONT OF A SHIP)** NAUTICAL TERM, CUTS THROUGH WATER, POINTED SHAPE	**BOW (WEAPON)** TOOL FOR SHOOTING ARROWS, REQUIRES SKILL, STRINGED
CLUB (ORGANIZATION) GROUP OF PEOPLE, COMMON INTEREST, MEMBERSHIP	**CLUB (WEAPON)** BLUNT, USED FOR HITTING, MADE OF WOOD OR METAL	**CLUB (NIGHTLIFE)** DANCING, MUSIC AND ENTERTAINMENT

7

Mission 5: The Ultimate Game Planner

"Hey guys, check this out!" I said, my voice bubbling with excitement as our avatars zipped into our digital playground. This time, it was transformed into a buzzing virtual sports arena, complete with cheering fans and flashing scoreboards.

Spencer decked out in a coach's outfit, complete with a whistle, was waiting for us with a soccer ball at his feet. "Guardians, ready to kick things up a notch?" he asked, his eyes sparkling with fun. "Here's a riddle to get us rolling: What can run all day but never gets tired?"

We all huddled together, throwing guesses back and forth. Hiro, tapping his chin thoughtfully, finally said, "Is it... a refrigerator?"

"You scored, Hiro!" Spencer cheered, kicking the soccer ball up into a digital goal that appeared out of nowhere. "This time, in 'The Ultimate Game,' you're diving into the world of sports and hobbies, with a special focus on our bionic buddy, Beni. You'll use AI for strategy, coaching, and learning new tricks. Think of AI as your personal sports and hobbies tutor, enhancing your skills and strategies."

My heart raced with excitement. "AI as a coach? This is gonna be awesome!" I exclaimed, imagining all the cool things we could do.

"Absolutely!" Spencer said, tossing the soccer ball from one hand to the other. "But first, Miss Fields has some game-changing lessons on data visualization and predictive analytics for you. Let's see how AI can turn you into top-notch players and hobbyists!"

With that, Spencer pointed us toward a door that shimmered like a gateway to a new world of adventure. "Off to Miss Fields' lab, Guardians! Let the games begin!"

• • • ● • ● • ● • •

We stepped through the door and found ourselves in a room that looked like a mix between a high-tech lab and a sports analyst's dream. Walls lined with screens showing soccer games, chess matches, and even a section with Beni the bionic hound doing tricks.

Miss Fields, wearing a referee's whistle around her neck, greeted us with a big smile. "Welcome, Guardians! Ready to explore how AI can turn you into sports and hobbies experts?"

Gabi leaned forward, her eyes wide with curiosity. "Like, can AI teach me how to paint better?"

"Exactly, Gabi!" Miss Fields replied. "AI can analyze your painting style and suggest techniques to improve. But first, let's start with data visualization in sports."

She pointed to a screen showing a soccer match. "See this? It's a heat map showing where players spend most of their time on the field. Red areas mean high activity. It's like a secret map revealing the team's strategy."

Hiro, always eager for the details, asked, "How does AI figure this out?"

"Great question, Hiro!" Miss Fields clicked to another screen showing a graph with peaks and valleys. "AI analyzes tons of game data – player movements, speeds, and even ball possession – and turns it into visual stories. Like this line graph shows a player's speed during a match."

"Now, let's talk about predictive analytics," she continued. "Does anyone know what that might mean?"

"Sure," Aakash answered confidently. "It's like making a guess about what is going to happen."

"Exactly," Miss Fields said, "AI doesn't just show us what happened; it predicts what could happen. Imagine it's like a chess game. AI can analyze past games and suggest your next best move."

Miss Fields then brought up a picture of Beni. "And for our pet-loving Guardians, AI can even help with your pets! It can learn Beni's behavior patterns and suggest new tricks or routines for his training."

Zara, who had given Beni a few robotic upgrades after I found and rescued him after a car accident, was thinking about Beni and asked, "Could AI help us understand why Beni barks at certain things?"

"Yes, Zara!" Miss Fields beamed. "AI can analyze Beni's barking patterns, maybe even predict what makes him anxious or excited. It's all about understanding the data."

Our heads were spinning with ideas as Miss Fields wrapped up. "Remember, Guardians, AI can enhance your skills, whether in sports, hobbies, or even understanding your pets better."

As we were about to leave, Miss Fields called us back. "Wait, Guardians! There's more to explore, especially about computer vision and the connection between robotics and AI."

We gathered around again, intrigued. Miss Fields brought up an image of a robotic arm painting a picture. "This," she said, "is where computer vision comes into play. It's an AI technology that helps machines 'see' and understand the visual world."

Gabi looked fascinated. "So, it's like giving AI eyes?"

"Exactly, Gabi!" Miss Fields pointed to the robotic arm. "Computer vision allows robots to interpret visual information, like colors and shapes, and even create art."

Zara, who loved anything to do with robotics, asked, "How does it work with AI?"

"Well, Zara," Miss Fields answered, "AI processes the visual data that the robot sees, helping it make decisions. For instance, if the robot is painting, AI helps it choose the right colors and strokes based on the image it sees."

Miss Fields then showed a video of Beni, the bionic hound, navigating an obstacle course. "Here, AI and robotics work together to help Beni move. Sensors and cameras help him 'see' his environment, and AI processes this information to guide his movements."

Hiro added, "So, AI can help Beni understand the world around him, like where to walk or when to jump?"

"Absolutely, Hiro!" Miss Fields replied. "AI gives Beni the information he needs to interact with his surroundings safely and effectively. It's a beautiful synergy between AI and robotics."

With our minds now brimming with new insights into computer vision, robotics, and AI, we felt more prepared than ever for the Ultimate Game. The possibilities of what we could do with this technology were endless, and we were eager to start experimenting.

· · ● · ● · ● · ● ·

"Welcome back, young Guardians!" Dr. Mooseroo said as she invited us into her workshop.

She handed each of us a sleek, futuristic-looking device. "This is the Visionary Lens," she explained, holding up one of the gadgets. "It's a computer vision tool that helps you understand and analyze visual data. Perfect for sports analytics and understanding Beni's movements."

Hiro, always eager to learn about new tech, examined the device closely. "So, this can help us see things like AI does?"

"Exactly, Hiro!" Dr. Mooseroo replied. "Imagine you're watching a soccer game. This lens can analyze players' movements, showing you patterns and strategies that might not be obvious at first glance."

Gabi, with a thoughtful look, asked, "Could it also help us create training programs for Beni?"

Dr. Mooseroo nodded enthusiastically. "Certainly! By analyzing Beni's movements, you can design exercises and routines that cater to his strengths and help him navigate better."

She then presented us with another tool, a tablet with an intricate app. "And this is the Strategy Synthesizer. It uses predictive analytics to help you devise game plans and strategies, whether for sports or helping Beni become more agile."

"So, we can use these tools to excel in sports and improve Beni's life?" Aakash asked, looking for the practical applications.

"You've got it!" Dr. Mooseroo affirmed. "These tools will give you insights into both the world of sports and the ways AI can enhance the capabilities of our robotic companions like Beni."

Equipped with the Visionary Lens and Strategy Synthesizer, we felt like we had the future of sports and AI-assisted pet care in our hands. The possibilities seemed limitless, and we were eager to see how we could apply these innovative tools in real-life scenarios.

"I understand you have an important mission ahead of you, Guardians. These only get more complex as you go- but I am certain you are going to succeed. Don't forget, AI is only a tool- it's your smarts and heart that will make the difference." With that, Dr. Mooseroo melted into the screen and was gone.

• • • • • ● • ● • • • •

The soccer field buzzed with energy as our team, armed with our AI insights, prepared for the biggest game of the season. Each of us had a role to play in this AI-driven adventure, and the excitement was palpable.

As we set up our equipment, Hiro, the tech genius among us, explained to the team how the AI would work. "This AI isn't just any coach; it's like having a super brain analyzing every move and giving us real-time tips!"

Some team members seemed unsure, their eyes darting between the AI setup and the familiar soccer field. Zara, ever the empath, sensed their hesitation. "Guys, it's cool! Think of it as gaining an extra edge, like having x-ray vision during the game!"

Demonstration day arrived, and the field transformed into a tech playground. We had set up a large screen showing live analytics powered by AI. Gabi orchestrated a showcase, demonstrating how the AI used computer vision to track and analyze player movements, predicting plays and suggesting improvements.

"Watch this," Gabi said, pointing to the screen as a player made a swift pass. The screen lit up, showing the trajectory and speed, and then offered a suggestion for a better passing angle. The players, initially skeptical, began to see the value, their eyes widening with each play.

Not everything was smooth sailing, though. We noticed the AI's advice seemed skewed towards the more experienced players. "We can't leave anyone behind," I reminded the team. "Let's tweak the AI to consider everyone's skills."

We spent hours feeding the AI with more data, including individual skill assessments. Slowly, the AI began offering personalized tips, encouraging less experienced players and challenging the veterans. The result was a team where everyone felt valued and included.

Our coach, Mr. Angelo, initially seemed wary of the AI. "Soccer is more than just data and algorithms," he muttered.

I approached him with a proposal. "Mr. Angelo, your experience is invaluable. How about we use AI as a tool to complement your coaching?"

Together, we found a balance. The AI provided data-driven insights, while Mr. Angelo used his experience for strategy and morale-boosting.

Beni, our bionic dog mascot, became a sensation. Equipped with sensors and AI, he interacted with the players, fetching balls and even participating in training drills. His playful presence was a reminder that AI could be fun and engaging.

On game day, our team was a fusion of human spirit and AI intelligence. The crowd cheered as our players, guided by AI insights, displayed remarkable teamwork and strategy.

The highlight came when our AI suggested an unexpected player for a critical penalty kick. The crowd held its breath as the ball soared into the net, a perfect goal. We had not only won the game but also won over the skeptics.

After the game, we gathered around, our faces beaming with pride. "We did it!" exclaimed Gabi. "We showed everyone how AI can bring out the best in us!"

Zara added, "It was more than just winning. We brought the team together, everyone got their moment to shine."

• • • • ● • ● • • •

Back in our virtual world, Spencer waited with a proud smile. "Guardians, you've demonstrated the power of AI in sports, but more importantly, you've shown how technology can enhance teamwork and inclusivity."

"What's next for us?" asked Hiro, eager for more.

Spencer's avatar shimmered with excitement. "Prepare for 'Healthcare Heroics.' You'll explore how AI is revolutionizing the medical field. The adventure continues!"

As we logged off, our hearts were full. The 'Ultimate Game Planner' mission was more than a project; it was a journey that taught us the true value of technology in bringing people together. With anticipation for our next mission, we stepped back into our world, ready to embrace the future of AI in healthcare.

Your Turn!

Who will win? You versus the AI!

Hey Quantum Kids! Ready for a fun challenge where you get to match wits with AI? In "Who Will Win: You vs. The AI," you'll test your sports prediction skills against an AI program. Let's see who comes out on top – your brain or the machine brain! Why This Activity Rocks:

- It's a blast to see if you can outsmart AI.

- You'll learn about probability, decision-making, and sports analytics.

- It demonstrates how AI uses data and context to make predictions.

- Plus, it's a great way to blend sports, fun, and learning!

What you need:

- The "Who Will Win: You vs. The AI" scenarios below

- Pen and paper

- Access to a generative AI program like ChatGPT or Bard (with adult supervision)

How-to:

1. Choose a Scenario: Pick a scenario card. Each card has a detailed sports situation with context that affects the outcome.

For example, "In a soccer game, Team A has been dominating possession and has just won a corner kick. Will they score from this corner?"

2. Make Your Prediction: Write down your prediction based on the scenario. Think about the context provided – it's not just a random guess! Consider factors like team performance, player skills, and game conditions.

3. Consult the AI: Type the scenario into the AI program and ask it to predict the outcome. For example, "Based on the given scenario in a soccer game, what is the likelihood of Team A scoring from the corner kick?"

4. Compare Predictions: Write down the AI's prediction next to yours. Does the AI agree with you, or does it have a different take on the situation?

5. Reveal the Outcome: Each scenario card has a predetermined outcome based on realistic probabilities. Check the answer and see who was closer – you or the AI!

6. Keep Score: If your prediction is closer to the actual outcome than the AI's, score a point. Keep track of points across multiple scenarios to see who's the ultimate predictor.

7. Reflection Time: After playing a few rounds, reflect on the experience. What strategies did you use for your predictions? How did the AI approach the problem? Did any results surprise you?

Remember! This game is about having fun and exploring AI's capabilities. Whether you score more points or the AI does, you're learning and having a great time – and that's what counts in the end! Now, gather your friends or family, grab those scenario cards, and let the predictions begin! Who knows, you might just be the next sports analytics whiz!

Scenarios

Scenario 1: Soccer Penalty Kick: A skilled striker known for accuracy is taking a penalty kick against an experienced goalkeeper with a high save rate.

Scenario 2: Basketball Free Throw: A basketball player with an 80% free-throw success rate is taking two shots.

Scenario 3: Tennis Tiebreak: In a tennis match, both players have equal win-loss records and similar playing styles entering a tiebreak.

Scenario 4: Chess Tournament: A seasoned chess player faces a newcomer with a surprising winning streak in a tournament.

Scenario 5: School Spelling Bee: Two finalists in a school spelling bee: one is known for their extensive vocabulary, the other for their calm under pressure.

Scenario 6: Running Race: In a 100-meter dash, one runner has consistently faster times in practice, but the other has recently improved significantly.

Scenario 7: Video Game Challenge: Two players compete in a popular video game. One has more experience, but the other has been practicing intensively for weeks.

Scenario 8: Cooking Competition: In a cooking competition, one contestant is a professional chef, while the other is a talented amateur with innovative recipes.

Scenario 9: Robotics Contest: Two teams compete in a robotics contest. One team has a more advanced robot, but the other team has a better strategy.

Scenario 10: Art Contest: Two artists enter a contest; one has years of experience, while the other is known for their unique, unconventional style.

These scenarios can be used to predict outcomes and compare your predictions with AI-generated ones. The goal is to understand how different factors influence the likelihood of various outcomes and how AI processes this information. You can find the outcomes suggested by AI in the answer key at the back of this book.

AI Eye Spy: The Collage Challenge

Hey there, AI Guardians! Have you ever seen those hilarious computer vision memes, like where an AI has to guess if it's looking at a dog or a bagel? Sometimes, they're spot on, and other times, well... let's just say AI still has a lot to learn! Today, we're going to dive into the world of computer vision with a super fun activity called "AI Eye Spy: The Collage Challenge" where you will explore how AI and computer vision work by creating and deciphering clever collages.

What you need:

- Magazines, newspapers, or printed images.

- Scissors and glue.

- Poster board or large paper for each participant.

- Markers or pens for labeling.

How-to:

Part 1: Create Your AI Puzzle

Collage Creation:

- Cut out various images – animals, objects, people, food, you name it!

- Create a collage on your poster board. Be creative! Arrange the images in a way that tells a story or just in a super cool design.

- Once done, give your collage a fun name that doesn't give away too much.

Play "AI Eye Spy":

- Share your collage with a friend or family member.

- Describe an item without saying what it is, like "I spy with my little eye, something that can fly but isn't a bird."

- Let them guess! This is how computer vision tries to identify objects based on descriptions.

Part 2: The Disguise Game

Trade and Transform:

- Swap collages with someone else.

- Now, each of you adds or changes three things in the other person's collage. Maybe put a hat on a cat or turn a car into a submarine!

- The trickier, the better - think like an AI trying to identify objects in unusual contexts.

Guess the Changes:

- Look at the transformed collage and try to spot the changes.

- Guess what the original images were before they were "disguised."

- This part of the game is like training an AI to recognize objects even when they look a little different than usual.

Discuss how this activity is similar to how AI systems, using computer vision, try to make sense of what they see. Sometimes AI gets it right, but other times, it can be tricked by changes in appearance or context, just like we were with our collages. It's a fun way to understand the challenges AI faces in interpreting the visual world! Remember, AI is learning just like us, and sometimes it sees a bagel when it's actually a dog!

Code-A-Hound: Training Beni in Scratch World

Hey AI Guardians! Ready to jump into the awesome world of coding? Today, we're going to explore Scratch, an incredibly fun and easy way to create your very own computer programs. And guess what? We're going to learn a little coding and create a special world where you'll train our favorite bionic hound, Beni!

What you need:

- A computer or tablet with internet access.

- A Scratch account (it's free and easy to set up at [scratch.mit. edu https://scratch.mit.edu/projects/editor/?tutorial=getSta rted].

How-to:

Getting Started with Scratch:

1. Explore Scratch: First, head to Scratch's website and play around with the "Getting Started" tutorial. It's a great way to learn the basics of how to make sprites (characters) move, jump, dance, and more.

2. Create Your Beni Sprite: Now, let's bring Beni into the Scratch world! You can create a sprite that looks like Beni. If you're feeling extra creative, customize Beni with some cool bionic features.

Building Beni's Training World:

1. Design the Setting: Create a background for Beni's training. This could be a park, an obstacle course, or anywhere you think a bionic hound would love to train.

2. Coding the Training: Use simple drag-and-drop blocks to code how Beni interacts with his world. Maybe Beni can fetch a ball when you click it, jump over obstacles, or even do a little dance when he's happy!

3. Add Challenges & Rewards: Make the game more interesting by adding challenges for Beni to complete. For each challenge he completes, you can code Beni to do a happy action or earn a 'treat.'

Sharing Your Game:

1. Test and Tweak: Play your game and see how Beni does. Is there anything you want to change or add? Maybe more challenges or a fun soundtrack

2. Share with Friends: Once you're happy with your game, share it with friends or family! They can help train Beni, too, and give you ideas for more cool features.

Reflect on how creating a game on Scratch is a lot like training a real pet. It takes patience, creativity, and sometimes a bit of trial and error to get things right. But most importantly, it's a whole lot of fun! Remember, every coder starts somewhere, and Scratch is an amazing first step into the world of programming. Who knows, maybe one day you'll create AI programs as cool as the ones we use in our Guardian missions!

8

Mission 6: Healthcare Heroics

As our avatars gathered again in the vibrant and ever-evolving world of "Guardians of AI," our environment transformed into an intricately detailed digital hospital. Amidst this high-tech medical backdrop stood Spencer, clad in a virtual lab coat.

"Total mad scientist vibe," Gabi whispered

"Totally!" I agreed

"Guardians, before we embark on today's healthcare mission, I have a little riddle for you," he said, his digital eyes twinkling. "I listen to the heart's secrets but don't have ears. I help reveal what's hidden inside, but I don't have eyes. What am I?"

We all huddled together, pondering over Spencer's riddle. It was Zara who lit up with realization first. "It's a stethoscope, isn't it?" she asked excitedly.

"Excellent, Zara! A stethoscope it is. Just like this tool helps doctors understand what's happening inside the body, you'll be using the tools of AI to delve into the world of healthcare, uncovering patterns and insights to keep everyone healthy."

Spencer's avatar paced slowly, his expression turning more serious. "As you would expect, with this being your second to last test, today's mission is considerably more critical than the five that have come before, Guardians. If there's one crucial lesson we've learned from the pandemic, it's the importance of quickly understanding and tracking diseases. The ability to rapidly analyze vast amounts of health data can be the difference between containment and a crisis."

He paused, allowing the weight of his words to sink in. "AI has played a pivotal role in monitoring and responding to health emergencies. It helps predict outbreaks, understand disease patterns, and even develop treatments and vaccines. Your challenge will be applying this knowledge to a scenario unfolding in our school."

Spencer's avatar gestured towards a door that shimmered into existence. "In the lab, Miss Fields will guide you through the intricacies of AI in healthcare. You'll learn how to harness this powerful tool to positively impact our community. Remember, what you learn today could be vital in safeguarding the health of those around you."

With a final nod, Spencer concluded, "Now, off to the lab, Guardians. Miss Fields awaits to equip you with the knowledge and tools you'll need for this vital mission. Good luck!"

· · · ● ● ● ● ● · ·

The door opened, revealing the bright, high-tech interior of the virtual lab, signaling the beginning of a new chapter in our journey as Guardians of AI.

As our avatars materialized inside the virtual hospital's high-tech lab, we found Miss Fields standing amidst a flurry of digital screens and holographic images. She looked every part the futuristic doctor, her avatar adorned with a lab coat and surrounded by representations of AI-driven medical breakthroughs.

"Welcome, Guardians, to the heart of AI in healthcare!" Miss Fields began, her voice echoing with excitement in the digital space. "Today, we're going to deepen our understanding of deep learning, explore structured and unstructured data in medicine, and see how AI helps predict health outcomes and aid in drug discovery."

Miss Fields started with an animated model of a neural network. "Deep learning is like giving AI a microscope to examine complex medical data," she explained. "These neural networks can analyze layers upon layers of information, learning patterns that even the most experienced doctors might miss."

She then displayed two types of medical records: a neatly organized chart (structured data) and a handwritten doctor's note with an X-ray image (unstructured data). "AI's ability to understand structured data, like this chart, and unstructured data, like these notes and images, is revolutionizing how we approach patient care."

"Our AI can predict health trends by analyzing patterns in vast amounts of medical data," Miss Fields continued, showing graphs of disease outbreaks and recovery rates. "It's like putting together a complex puzzle, where each piece of data helps foresee potential health crises."

As Miss Fields began to discuss drug discovery, her virtual lab transformed into a dynamic, interactive space filled with holographic images of molecules and AI algorithms at work.

"Think of AI in drug discovery like a super-smart chef trying to create a new recipe," Miss Fields explained, her avatar pointing to the floating molecules. "Just like a chef mixes different ingredients to make a delicious dish, AI experiments with various chemical compounds to find new medicines."

She brought up a familiar example. "You know how some of you take medicine for allergies or colds? All of those medicines started as an idea and went through lots of testing to ensure it was safe and worked well. AI can speed up this process by quickly testing many different ideas to see which might make the best new medicine."

Zara's avatar stepped forward, her expression thoughtful. "Miss Fields, does that mean AI could help find medicines for diseases common in places like my home country, Nigeria?"

"Absolutely, Zara!" Miss Fields replied enthusiastically. "AI can be used globally, including for diseases more common in certain parts of the world. It's like giving doctors and scientists a helping hand to find cures faster."

Zara's eyes lit up with realization. "So, by learning AI, I could help find new treatments for people back home. I could be a part of creating those cures!"

"Yes, Zara, that's exactly right," Miss Fields encouraged. "With AI, you can contribute to global health, no matter where you are. You could be a healer, not just in Nigeria but for the whole world."

Inspired by this revelation, Zara joined her teammates in the interactive exercise, feeding different types of medical data into the AI model. As they worked, each of them saw the potential impact of their learning – not just in the virtual world but in real communities across the globe.

Wrapping up, Miss Fields said, "Today's exploration of AI in health-care shows us the potential of technology not only to treat but also predict and prevent illnesses. I have a good friend who has even used AI to predict when chronic kidney disease might worsen in patients. His work allows doctors to stay ahead of the disease and families to have more quality time with their loved ones. As you embark on your 'Healthcare Heroics' mission, remember the power of AI to change lives for the better!"

We were just about to log out when Miss Fields stopped us. "Kids! I almost forgot, can you take this to Dr. Mooseroo?" she asked, handing me a beaker filled with a bubbling, luminescent liquid.

"What is it?" I asked, my eyes wide with curiosity as I gently took the beaker.

"That," Miss Fields said, her voice tinged with excitement, "just might be part of a cure for cancer. Our AI model discovered it earlier this morning. It's a compound that the AI predicted could stop the growth of cancer cells. We're still in the early stages, but it's a promising start."

My hands trembled slightly, holding the beaker. "This is incredible," I whispered, amazed by the significance of the liquid in my hands.

"Yes, it is," Miss Fields agreed, her eyes reflecting the liquid's glow. "But it needs further analysis. Dr. Mooseroo's lab is equipped with advanced tools for just that. She'll conduct the next set of tests to verify the AI's predictions."

Zara looked on, her eyes brimming with pride and wonder. "This is what we're learning about? We're part of something this big?"

"Indeed, you are," Miss Fields nodded. "Every lesson, every exercise you do here, contributes to real-world advancements like this. What you learn could one day change the world."

We nodded, the sense of responsibility and excitement growing within us. Carefully, I carried the beaker out of Miss Fields' lab and towards Dr. Mooseroo's workshop, each step filled with the potential of what our learning could lead to.

• • • • • ● • ● • • •

Dr. Mooseroo greeted us with a warm smile. Her eyes lit up as I carefully handed her the beaker from Miss Fields.

"Ah, the potential cancer treatment," Dr. Mooseroo said, her voice filled with reverence and excitement as she took the beaker. "This is a prime example of how AI can lead us to breakthroughs that were once mere dreams. I'll handle this with the utmost care. Thank you, Vivian."

She placed the beaker safely in a secure containment unit. Then she turned to us, her demeanor shifting to focus on our immediate mission. "Now, for your task at hand. The stomach bug outbreak at your school is a pressing matter, and I've prepared just the right tools for you to address it."

Dr. Mooseroo led us to a bench where several sleek, digital toolkits lay in neat rows. She handed each of us a kit. "This," she explained, lifting a device that resembled a high-tech tablet, "is your Pattern Predictor. It's designed to analyze health data, spot trends in illness outbreaks, and help you predict where the bug might hit next."

Next, she presented a device resembling a pair of futuristic goggles. "And this is your Neural Network Navigator. It'll give you an insight into how AI learns about diseases, visualizing the complex process of neural networks. It's crucial for understanding and identifying disease patterns."

Zara, carefully examining the Neural Network Navigator, looked thoughtful. "So, we're using these to track the spread of the stomach bug and stop it before it affects more students?"

"Exactly," Dr. Mooseroo replied. "You'll be applying your AI knowledge to real-world health monitoring. Think of yourselves as data detectives, using these tools to safeguard your school community."

We each took our toolkit, feeling a sense of responsibility and excitement. Armed with AI technology and a newfound understanding of its capabilities, we were ready to tackle the challenge ahead, determined to make a difference in our school.

• • • ● • ● • ● • •

As we gathered in the school library to plan our mission, Zara raised a crucial point with her natural empathy. "Before we start collecting any data about the stomach bug, we need to make sure we have everyone's permission. It's like asking if it's okay to borrow someone's pencil before taking it."

"That's right," I added, recalling our lessons from Miss Fields. "And we need to be super careful with this information. It's not just regular school stuff; it's about people's health. It's like having a secret someone tells you; you don't share it with anyone else."

We decided to start by talking to the school nurse. She was impressed with our initiative but also reminded us about the importance of patient consent. "Just like doctors need permission to share your health information, you need to make sure students and their families are okay with using this data," she explained.

"Think of getting consent as getting the code to a secret club," Hiro said later as we discussed the nurse's advice. "You can't just let anyone in; they need to know and agree to the club's rules."

Even with parent and student consent to share the data, we faced an unexpected challenge: misinformation. Rumors about the stomach bug began to spread, causing panic among students.

"Looks like we've got another problem to solve," Gabi said as we discussed this new development.

Taking the lead again, Zara suggested, "We need to use our AI model to debunk these myths and provide accurate information."

We quickly adapted our AI program to analyze and counter the rumors with factual data. We even created an infographic shared in classrooms and on the school's social media.

Armed with this understanding, we approached our data collection thoughtfully. We prepared a simple explanation of our project and how the data would be used, ensuring it was easy for everyone to understand. We then asked students and their parents for permission to include their data in our study.

Aakash suggested we use a secure database to ensure the data's security. "It's like a treasure chest that only we have the key to," he said. "Only we can see the information, and we make sure it's locked away safely after we use it."

This approach not only helped us gain the trust of our school community but also taught us a valuable lesson in respecting and protecting sensitive information.

Our efforts paid off. The stomach bug spread was contained, and the misinformation was quelled. Our school community was grateful for our proactive approach, and we felt a sense of pride in our real-world impact.

Reflecting on our success, Zara said, "We've not only helped keep our friends healthy but also learned how important it is to respect everyone's privacy and keep their information safe."

• • • • ● • ● • • •

As our avatars regrouped with Spencer, the digital hospital faded, giving way to a serene park in the virtual world, symbolizing the harmony we had brought to our school community. Spencer stood there, beaming with pride.

"Guardians, you've surpassed expectations," he began, his voice full of admiration. "Your work with TutorBot and managing the stomach bug outbreak at school has shown exceptional growth in your understanding of AI's capabilities and responsibilities."

Gabi, her avatar sitting on a digital bench, chimed in, "It's like we're not just learning about AI; we're learning how to use it to help people."

Hiro nodded, adding, "And how to make sure we use it in the right way. It's more than just coding and data; it's about understanding people's needs."

Spencer nodded approvingly. "Exactly, Hiro. AI is a powerful tool, but it's how you use it that truly makes a difference. Now, for your final mission – 'The Quantum Conundrum.' This will be your most challenging yet rewarding journey. You'll delve into the realms of quantum computing and AI, focusing on kindness and empathy."

Aakash raised an eyebrow. "Quantum computing and kindness? That's an unusual combination."

Spencer's avatar smiled mysteriously. "You'll see how they interconnect. Quantum computing's immense power can be harnessed for great good, but it requires a deep understanding of its impact on people and the world. Your mission is to use this advanced technology to solve a complex problem that affects your community, demonstrating how kindness and technology can work hand in hand."

"So it's about using this incredible technology responsibly and for the benefit of others." Zara offered.

"Exactly, Zara," Spencer replied. "You've all shown great potential in using AI to make positive changes. Now, it's time to take it a step further with quantum computing. Remember, the choices you make in this mission will shape the kind of AI guardians you'll become."

We looked at each other, excitement and determination in our virtual eyes. This final mission wasn't just another challenge; it was our chance to prove how far we'd come and how we could use our knowledge to make a real difference.

With a final nod from Spencer, our avatars stepped onto a new path, the virtual landscape transforming into a world of quantum processors and glowing circuits. The Quantum Conundrum awaited, and we were ready for the challenge.

Your Turn!

Build Your Own Neural Network Model

"Hey there, young Guardians of AI! Ready to become brilliant brain builders? Today, we're going to create our very own Neural Network Model. But don't worry, you won't need a supercomputer—just some everyday craft supplies and your amazing imagination!"

What you need:

- Colored paper or cardboard

- Strings or yarn of different colors

- Beads or buttons

- Glue or tape

- Markers or crayons

How-to:

1. Create Your Neurons: First, we're going to make our neurons. Think of neurons like tiny, brainy superheroes in your AI model. Each neuron can learn a small part of a big puzzle. Cut out small circles from your colored paper – these are your neurons. You can make as many as you like, depending on how big you want your network to be.

2. Link Your Neurons with Synapses: Now, let's connect these neurons with synapses. In the real brain, synapses are like phone

lines between neurons, sending messages back and forth. Use strings or yarn to connect your paper neurons. Glue one end of a string to a neuron and connect the other to a different neuron. Mix and match colors for a fun effect!

3. Add Your Data Points: Every neural network needs data to learn. Let's add some! Stick beads or buttons onto some neurons. These represent the data points that the network will use to learn and make predictions.

4. Label Your Network: Give your network a cool name and label the parts. You can name it anything – like 'BrainyNet' or 'Super-Thinker!' Use markers or crayons to write your network's name and label the neurons (input, hidden, and output layers).

5. Share Your Creation: Share your model with friends or family once you're done. Explain how each part works and what it represents. Teach them about neural networks and AI!

Congratulations! You've just built your very own neural network model. By creating this model, you've learned how AI can connect lots of small pieces of information to make smart decisions. Just like your network connects beads and neurons, AI connects data to help solve problems. Keep exploring and building, and remember, the world of AI is as limitless as your creativity!

AI Role-Play: Medical Edition

Hello, future AI doctors! Today, we're going to step into the shoes of an AI system in a doctor's office. Just like a doctor helps us when we're sick, AI can help doctors figure out what's wrong when we don't feel well. But remember, you're the AI in this game, so put on your thinking caps and get ready to solve some medical mysteries!

What you need:

- Index cards or small pieces of paper

- Markers or pens

- A 'Patient Symptoms' list

- A 'Disease Database' (a simple list of common illnesses and their symptoms, like stomach flu, strep throat, flu, a sprained ankle, etc.)

How-to:

1. Prepare Your Patient Cards: Let's start by making some patient cards. On each card, write down different symptoms that someone might have. For example, one card could say 'sore throat, fever, headache,' which might mean strep throat. Prepare several cards, each with a different set of symptoms. There is a starter list below, or you can make your own.

2. Create Your Disease Database: Now, make a list of common illnesses and their typical symptoms. This is your AI's 'database'

to refer to when making a diagnosis. You can use simple terms like 'Stomach Flu: upset stomach, vomiting, fever' or 'Sprained Ankle: swelling, pain, difficulty walking.'

3. Play the Role of AI: Time to play AI! Pick a patient card and read the symptoms. Now, use your disease database to figure out what illness they might have. Remember, just like real AI, you're using the information you have (the symptoms) to make your best guess.

4. Discuss Your Diagnosis: After you make a diagnosis, discuss it with your friends or family. Why did you think it was that illness? Was there another illness with similar symptoms? This is like how AI learns – by comparing information and making educated guesses.

Role-Play Variations: For a fun twist, you can also role-play as the patient, and someone else can be the AI, or you can even pretend to be a doctor using AI to help make the diagnosis!

Great job, AI doctors! Through this activity, you've learned how AI can help in understanding health problems by looking at symptoms, just like a real doctor. AI in healthcare is all about using information to help people feel better, and now you've seen firsthand how that works. Keep exploring, and who knows – maybe one day, you'll help invent new ways for AI to keep us healthy!"

Symptom Bank: Sore Throat, Fever, Cough, Stomach Pain, Nausea or Vomiting, Rash, Headache, Fatigue, Swelling in a Body Part, Difficulty Breathing, Loss of Appetite, Runny or Stuffy Nose

Illness Scenarios

1. Common Cold: Runny or Stuffy Nose, Cough, Sore Throat

2. Stomach Flu (Gastroenteritis): Stomach Pain, Nausea, Vomiting

3. Influenza (Flu): Fever, Headache, Fatigue, Cough

4. Strep Throat: Sore Throat, Fever, Headache

5. Allergic Reaction: Rash, Swelling, Difficulty Breathing

6. Migraine: Severe Headache, Nausea, Sensitivity to Light

7. Sprained Ankle: Swelling in Ankle, Pain, Difficulty Walking

8. Asthma: Difficulty Breathing, Cough, Wheezing

Sample Role-Play Scenario:

Patient Card: The patient is experiencing a headache, nausea, and sensitivity to light.

AI Diagnosis: Based on the symptoms, the AI predicts the patient might be experiencing a Migraine.

Discussion: Why might it be a migraine? Are there other illnesses with similar symptoms? Could it be a tension headache or something else? Let's check our disease database and see if the symptoms match better with another illness.

Disease Detective Scavenger Hunt

Hey there, young sleuths! Ready to put on your detective hats? Today, you're going to become disease detectives, tracking down clues to stop the spread of an illness. Just like real health experts use patterns to track diseases, you'll use clues to solve this medical mystery!

What you need:

- Clue Cards (prepared beforehand with symptoms or disease-related hints)

- Disease cards with names of common childhood illnesses (like Chickenpox, Flu, Stomach Bug)

- A map of your "investigation area" (like a classroom, house, or backyard)

- A prize or treat for the successful detectives

- A few of your siblings or friends to play along

How-to:

1. Prepare Your Clues: First, create cards describing different symptoms or hints about the disease. For example, one card could say, 'Lots of sneezes and a runny nose!' which might hint at the common cold. Hide these clues around your investigation area. If you need some ideas, there are some examples below.

2. Set the Scene: Tell the kids that there's been an outbreak of

a mystery illness, and it's up to them to figure out what it is and how to stop it. Give them the first clue to start their investigation."

3. Start the Scavenger Hunt: Kids will follow the clues, each leading to the next. Along the way, they'll gather information about the disease's symptoms.

4. Solve the Mystery: At the final clue, place a 'Disease' card that names the illness they've been tracking. The kids can then match the symptoms they found to the disease.

5. Debrief and Reward: Once they've solved the mystery, have a debrief session. A debrief is like when you sit down after doing something important, like playing a game or finishing a school project, and talk about what happened. It's like when you finish playing a soccer match and then sit with your team to talk about how the game went. You discuss what you did well, what could be better next time, and how everyone felt about it. It helps everyone understand and learn from the experience so you can do even better next time! To Discuss how each clue helped identify the disease and why it's important to recognize these signs in real life.

6. Reward your young disease detectives with a small prize or treat for their excellent sleuthing skills!

Bonus Tips for an Engaging Scavenger Hunt:

- Add pictures or drawings to your clues to make them more engaging and easier to understand for younger kids you might be playing with.

- Use a mix of obvious and slightly more challenging hiding spots to keep the game exciting but not too difficult.

- Ensure all hiding spots are safe and accessible for kids- like don't put a clue high up on a bookshelf where your younger brother might think to climb!

- Be ready to offer hints if your friends get stuck to keeping the game flowing and enjoyable.

Congratulations, detectives! You've just solved a medical mystery. Following the clues and using pattern recognition has taught you how health experts track diseases to keep everyone safe. Remember, being observant and understanding patterns are key skills in solving mysteries, whether in a game or real life. Great job!"

Sample Clue Set for Common Cold:

Clue #1: "I start with a tickle in your throat!"

- Hiding Suggestion: Tape this clue under a chair or a desk where it's slightly visible. It's an easy starting point that kicks off the hunt.

Clue #2: "Next, you might feel a bit stuffy here," with a drawing of a nose.

- Hiding Suggestion: Place this clue near a box of tissues or somewhere in a bathroom, connecting the location to the clue's theme.

Clue #3: "Sneezes coming in threes, achoo, achoo, achoo!"

- Hiding Suggestion: Hide this clue near a door or window, maybe tucked into the frame, to represent the air spreading the sneezes.

Clue #4: "Feeling chilly? You might have a fever."

- Hiding Suggestion: This clue can be near a thermostat or in a fridge (if it's safe and appropriate), symbolizing the change in temperature.

Clue #5: "When you're sick, rest is best!"

- Hiding Suggestion: The perfect spot for this clue is in a cozy area, like under a pillow on a couch or a resting spot, emphasizing the need for rest.

Clue #6: Final Clue/Disease Card: "You've tracked all the symptoms of the Common Cold!"

- Hiding Suggestion: The final clue should lead to a more challenging spot, like inside a book about health or in a play doctor's kit, if available.

9

Mission 7: The Quantum Conundrum

In the colorful, futuristic world of our RoboRumble quantum-scape, we gathered around Spencer, ready to receive instructions for our final mission. He stood there with a welcoming smile, but this time, the scene behind him was blank. No futuristic buildings, no neon schools, no high-tech hospitals.

"Welcome back, Guardians! Today, you embark on a special mission, one that combines the wonders of AI and quantum science with something much closer to home."

"Is this another one of your famous riddles, Spencer?" Hiro asked with a grin.

Spencer chuckled. "Not this time, Hiro. This is about something real, something that affects real people in our community. It's your final test, but think of it more as a new beginning."

Zara, her eyes reflecting the virtual glow, added, "So, we're using what we've learned to help others? That sounds important but also... kind of fun."

"Exactly, Zara," Spencer replied, nodding. "You'll first dive deeper into quantum computing here, with Miss Fields and Dr. Mooseroo guiding you. They'll show you the ropes, not just the 'how' but also the 'why' of using technology with care and empathy."

Aakash, pondered aloud, "So, it's not just about the tech, but how we use it to make a real difference?"

"You've got it, Aakash," said Spencer. "There's a shelter in our town, a place that offers hope and help to many, and it's facing tough times. Your challenge is to use your new skills to help keep that hope alive. It's about more than just solving problems; it's about understanding and caring for the people behind them."

We all nodded. It was clear that this was more than a game; it was a chance to make a positive impact in the real world.

"Remember, in the quantum world, things are interconnected in ways we can't always see," Spencer continued with a smile. "Just like in our world, where every act of kindness, every thoughtful use of technology, can make a big difference. Now, off you go to the quantum lab. Miss Fields is waiting to start this exciting journey with you."

As we gathered in the quantumscape, prepared for our lesson with Miss Fields, Spencer suddenly appeared with an unexpected instruction.

"Guardians, there's been a slight change in plan," he announced. "Before you dive into quantum computing with Miss Fields, you need to visit Dr. Mooseroo. She has something special for you, something essential for today's mission."

We exchanged surprised looks. Hiro, always curious about new gadgets, asked, "What kind of special something, Spencer?"

Spencer gave a wink. "Let's just say Dr. Mooseroo has developed a new tool, a prototype that's never been tested before. It's designed to enhance your understanding and application of quantum concepts in real time. Think of it as a key to unlocking the full potential of today's lesson and your mission."

Intrigued, Zara added, "So, we're like beta testers for a brand-new quantum invention? That sounds amazing!"

"Exactly, Zara," Spencer replied. "This tool will not only aid you in today's lesson but will also be crucial in applying what you learn to help the shelter in your community. It's a unique opportunity to experience the cutting-edge of quantum technology firsthand."

With a wave of his hand, a new portal opened, leading to Dr. Mooseroo's workshop. We stepped through, eager to discover what this new tool was and how it would shape our understanding of quantum computing.

• • • • ● • ● • • • •

In Dr. Mooseroo's workshop, filled with the usual gadgets and displays, the air buzzed with anticipation.

"Welcome, Guardians!" Dr. Mooseroo beamed. "I'm excited to introduce you to the Quantum Wristband, a revolutionary device that interacts with your environment and enhances learning."

She handed each of us a sleek wristband. "This device," she explained, "will help you visualize and understand quantum concepts in real time.

It's also equipped with AI that adapts to each of your learning styles, making complex ideas more accessible."

Vivi, fastening the wristband, joked, "Does it also come with a feature to untangle my ADHD thoughts like that quantum entanglement thing Miss Field's is going to tell us about?"

Dr. Mooseroo chuckled. "Well, it might just help you focus those brilliant thoughts of yours, Vivi. Think of it as a guide through the quantum world."

We each experimented with the wristbands, fascinated by how they displayed holographic images and data in response to our questions and movements. It was clear that these devices would be invaluable in our mission.

"Now, equipped with these Quantum Wristbands, you're ready for your lesson with Miss Fields," Dr. Mooseroo said, her eyes twinkling with excitement. "They'll give you a hands-on experience with quantum computing like never before."

• • • ● • ● • ● • ●

As we stepped through the portal, we found ourselves in the quantum lab, a space filled with holographic images of atoms and colorful light particles.

"Hi, everyone! Ready to dive into the world of quantum computing?" Miss Fields asked, her eyes sparkling with excitement.

"Yes, but can you make it a bit simple for us?" Gabi said with a giggle.

"Of course, Gabi!" Miss Fields responded. She pointed to a hologram displaying a spinning coin. "Let's start with bits. In regular computers, bits are like light switches – either on or off, one or zero. But in quantum computers, we have qubits."

Hiro, furrowing his brow in concentration, looked at Miss Fields. "What exactly is a qubit?"

Miss Fields, always ready with an analogy, smiled and held up a holographic image of a spinning coin. "Think of a qubit, Hiro, like this coin. In classical computing, a bit is like a coin that's either heads or tails – on or off. But a qubit, in the quantum world, can be in a state of heads, tails, or both at the same time. This state is what we call superposition."

She saw the puzzled looks and added, "Imagine playing a video game where you can have a power-up that lets you be in two places at once. Superposition is like that ultimate power-up. It allows quantum computers to explore many possibilities simultaneously, making them incredibly powerful."

Zara, her curiosity piqued, chimed in. "So, it's like seeing the whole game board instead of just one path?"

"Exactly, Zara," Miss Fields responded with an approving nod. "Now, let's talk about entanglement. It's another key concept in quantum computing." She switched the hologram to show two particles spinning in sync. "When qubits become entangled, the state of one is directly related to the state of the other, no matter how far apart they are. It's as if they're invisibly connected."

Gabi, always looking for practical applications, asked, "How does that help in real life?"

"Well, Gabi, entanglement means information can be shared between qubits instantly," explained Miss Fields. "This can be used for things like ultra-secure communication or solving complex problems that traditional computers struggle with."

Aakash, always looking to delve deeper, wondered, "So, entanglement helps quantum computers process information in a way that's not just faster but also different from how regular computers work?"

"Yes, Aakash! It's not just about speed; it's about a whole new way of processing information," Miss Fields concluded, her eyes gleaming with excitement. "That's the magic of quantum computing."

Miss Fields had just finished explaining entanglement, but I wasn't sure I was following. I had been fidgeting with my quantum wristband and was afraid I had missed something, "So if I get this right, entanglement is like my ADHD – everything's somehow connected, and when one thought pops up, a bunch of others follow, no matter how far off they seem?"

The group burst into laughter, and Miss Fields chuckled. "Well, Vivi, that's one way to put it! Entanglement does indeed show how things can be interconnected in unexpected ways. Your thought process might just be the perfect example of how multiple ideas can be linked, much like entangled qubits affecting each other."

Miss Fields concluded with a smile, "See, everyone brings a unique perspective to understanding quantum computing. Vivi's imaginative analogy reminds us that sometimes, thinking outside the box – or outside the conventional bit – can lead to brilliant insights."

As if reading my mind, Aakash questioned, "How does this help with real-world problems?"

"Well, Aakash, because quantum computers can process and analyze huge amounts of data much faster than traditional computers. This makes them incredibly powerful for solving complex problems, like optimizing resources for the shelter."

Gabi, connecting the dots, said, "So, we can use quantum computing to look at the shelter's needs in a whole new way?"

"That's the spirit, Gabi!" Miss Fields beamed. "And remember, it's not just about the technology. It's about how you use it to make positive changes. With quantum computing, you can innovate solutions that are more efficient, more effective, and more aligned with real human needs."

• • • • ● • ● • • •

In Mr. Cowley's social studies class, the buzz of conversation fell silent as he announced our new project. "This assignment is about more than grades. It's about making an impact in our community," he explained, his eyes scanning the room.

Gabi leaned forward to ask, "What kind of project, Mr. Cowley?"

"A group project on community service," he replied. "You'll choose a local issue or organization to support. Think about what really matters to you and your community. Nothing is off limits as long as you go and make a difference." He dismissed us to work in our groups at the library, where we could brainstorm ideas.

We scoured the internet for ideas. Gabi's eyes widened as she read a headline aloud," 'Harmony Hill Shelter at Risk of Closure.' Guys, this could be it. This must be the shelter Spencer was telling us about. We can't let this happen.""

We leaned in, reading the article detailing the shelter's financial struggles and the vital support it provided to the community. The room was quiet, save for the soft hum of the computer, as the gravity of the situation sunk in. It was Aakash who broke the silence, his voice usually lively, now softened with a seriousness we seldom heard.

"My cousin... he stayed at Harmony Hill once," he shared, not meeting our eyes. "After his family lost their home, the shelter... it was their lifeline. They helped him and his family get back on their feet."

We turned to Aakash, seeing a new vulnerability in his usually upbeat demeanor. His story brought a human face to the issue, transforming the words on the screen into a reality that one of us had lived through.

Zara reached out, placing a gentle hand on Aakash's shoulder. "Then we have to help them," she said firmly. "It's not just a shelter; it's a place that gives hope, like it did for your cousin."

Hiro nodded in agreement, his hacker mind already ticking. "We could use our skills, the stuff we've learned about AI and quantum computing. Maybe there's a way to help them manage resources better or even raise funds."

The decision was unanimous without any further discussion. Our mission was set – we were going to help Harmony Hill shelter. It was no longer just a school project; it had become personal, a cause we all felt deeply connected to.

The following Saturday, we visited the shelter. The building, though worn, radiated hope.

For most of us, our visit to the Harmony Hill shelter was like stepping into a different world – one where each face held a story and the walls echoed with both struggle and strength. The shelter was modest, its walls adorned with drawings and messages of hope. The air was filled with a sense of community that was almost tangible.

As we walked through the shelter, we were greeted with cautious smiles from the residents. Their eyes told stories of hardship, but their smiles spoke of the resilience and warmth that the shelter nurtured. We sat down with a few of them, listening intently as they shared their journeys. Each story was a tapestry of challenges and triumphs, painting a picture of the shelter not just as a building but as a vital heartbeat of the community.

Amidst the chatter and occasional laughter, we met Mrs. Moore, a volunteer bustling around with an infectious energy. Her story was one of transformation – from a resident in her time of need to a beacon of hope for others. She shared how the shelter had given her a second chance at life and how she was now determined to pay it forward.

"You know," Mrs. Moore said, pausing her work to look at us with earnest eyes, "this place is more than just walls and beds. It's about community, about giving and receiving help. And you, with your fresh ideas and understanding of technology, you could really make a difference here."

Her words struck a chord in us. The idea of using our knowledge of AI and quantum computing to contribute something meaningful to the shelter sparked a wave of excitement. We saw potential solutions in every corner – from optimizing space to setting up efficient resource management systems.

"Combining technology and community can create miracles here," Mrs. Moore continued, her voice firm yet hopeful. "And I believe you are the right ones to make it happen."

Back at school, we gathered, buzzing with ideas. "We can use AI to optimize the shelter's resources, maybe even start a fundraising campaign," Aakash suggested, his fingers drumming on the table.

"And let's not forget about comfort and dignity," Zara added. "It's their home right now, after all. I feel like I am learning so much. I had no idea that many of the people here are unhoused because they have not had access to the things they need for brain health issues like bipolar depression or substance use disorder. If we can remember that being unhoused is sometimes a medical issue, maybe we can do more than make this a place to stay; we can make it a place to get support and services."

"Wow," I added thoughtfully. "I guess the work we did in the last mission is more important than I realized. My mom has bipolar disorder. I guess we better get to work!"

Equipped with our Quantum Wristbands and inspired by our lessons with Miss Fields and Dr. Mooseroo, we dove into the challenge. Aakash analyzed data to optimize space. Gabi sketched out new layouts, her drawings a kaleidoscope of color.

Zara and I worked on a digital campaign, our messages crafted to touch hearts and open wallets. "This isn't just a shelter; it's a beacon of hope," Zara typed, her words powerful and true.

Hiro and Zara talked with the residents, ensuring our plans aligned with their needs. "Your voices matter most," Zara assured them.

Our efforts transformed the shelter. The space became more efficient, and the atmosphere more welcoming. Fueled by our community's generosity, the fundraising campaign exceeded all expectations.

Standing outside the shelter, now a hub of hope and activity, we felt a massive sense of accomplishment. "We didn't just use technology. We put our hearts into this," Gabi reflected. "As Spencer told us, 'In a world filled with code, kindness is the ultimate key.'"

Mr. Cowley's words echoed in our hearts as we looked at the thriving shelter, "It's about making an impact." And that's precisely what we, the Guardians of Harmony Hill, had achieved. We left the shelter that day as tech-savvy kids and as young guardians of our community, ready to use our knowledge and skills to continue making a positive impact in Harmony Hill and beyond.

· · · · ● · ● · · ·

In the RoboRumble quantumscape, a celebration was underway. Our avatars stood in a circle, surrounded by Spencer, Dr. Mooseroo, and Miss Fields. The virtual environment was abuzz with the vibrant colors and sounds of a festive gathering.

Spencer stepped forward, his voice filled with pride. "Guardians, today is not just a celebration of completing your mission. It's a recognition of how far you've come. You've shown that you're not just learners of AI and quantum computing but real helpers in your families, schools, and communities."

Dr. Mooseroo, her eyes twinkling behind her spectacles, added, "You've used technology not as a mere tool but as a means to bring about positive change. You've proven that compassion and innovation go hand in hand."

Miss Fields, her smile as warm as ever, continued, "You've embraced the complexities of AI and quantum computing and applied them in ways that truly matter. You've shown that you're ready to be the future guardians of AI."

Spencer nodded, gesturing to the world around them. "This quantum-scape was just the beginning. The real world, with all its challenges and opportunities, is where you'll make your mark. Remember, AI is evolving, just like you. By using it regularly and thoughtfully, you can help shape it into a force for good."

He paused, letting his words sink in. "AI, like any tool, reflects the values and data we feed it. It's important to be part of this evolution, to ensure it's trained on fair and equitable data, and that its uses are beneficial for everyone."

Gabi, her eyes shining with determination, spoke up. "We won't just sit on the sidelines. We'll be part of shaping a future where technology is used with kindness and responsibility."

Hiro added enthusiastically, "And we'll make sure it's fun, too! We're ready to be the guardians, the ones who make sure AI helps everyone."

Zara summed up the sentiment, "We're not just the future guardians of AI; we're the guardians of our community and each other."

The mentors applauded, and the quantumscape lit up with celebratory fireworks. As we watched, a sense of responsibility and excitement for the future filled us. We were ready to step into the world, not just as kids who had learned about AI and quantum computing but as young guardians ready to use our knowledge and hearts to make a difference.

As the celebration began to quiet down in the quantumscape, Spencer left us with a parting thought that stuck with me. "Guardians," he said, "remember, every click shapes tomorrow."

I turned to Aakash, feeling the weight and excitement of Spencer's words. "It's kind of amazing, isn't it, Aakash? Every click shapes tomorrow. It makes me think about how every decision we make, especially with technology, is shaping our future."

Aakash nodded, his eyes reflecting a sense of understanding. "You're right, Vivian. What we've learned here about AI and quantum com puting... it's not just cool tech stuff. It's about making choices that build a better tomorrow."

I couldn't help but smile, thinking about the journey we had been on. "We're more than just kids playing with gadgets. We're guardians, shaping how AI grows and is used. It's like we have the power to program a better world."

"And the cool part is," Aakash added, "we're not waiting until we grow up to make a difference. Look at what we did for the Harmony Hill shelter! We're already on our way to making that better tomorrow."

"Yeah," I said, my mind racing with possibilities. "And we won't stop here. We'll keep exploring, keep experimenting. Who knows what other challenges we can tackle next? Maybe we can inspire others to use AI for good, too."

Aakash's smile broadened. "Exactly! We're like gardeners, tending to the tech tree, making sure it grows in the right directions."

Laughing, I replied, "A tech tree, huh? I like that. Branches reaching out to all sorts of amazing places!"

As Aakash and I rejoined the others, leaving the Quantumscape behind, I felt a surge of purpose and anticipation. We were stepping into the real world not just as students who had completed a project but as young visionaries ready to embrace and shape the future – a future we would help mold with every click, every choice, and every dream.

Your Turn!

Quantum Entanglement Card Trick

Hey Quantum Magicians! Welcome to a world where magic and science intertwine, creating illusions that will boggle the mind and reveal the wonders of quantum mechanics! Today, you're not just young scientists; you're Quantum Magicians about to perform a trick that will dazzle and teach all at once.

In the mysterious realm of quantum physics, there's a fascinating phenomenon known as 'entanglement' – a kind of magical connection where two particles, no matter how far apart, seem to communicate instantly. But how can this mind-bending concept be shown in a fun and understandable way? With a deck of cards, of course!

You're about to learn and perform the Quantum Entanglement Card Trick. It's not just any card trick; it's a journey into the heart of quantum weirdness, where you'll make it seem like two separate decks of cards are eerily connected – mimicking the phenomenon of entanglement.

So, gather your decks, sharpen your magician's flair, and get ready to step into the shoes of a Quantum Magician. Let's shuffle reality and illusion together and show your audience how the quantum world can be as magical as any spell or potion!

Are you ready to amaze and educate? Let's get started, Quantum Magicians!

What you need:

- Two decks of playing cards.

- A bag or a box to conceal one deck.

How-to:

1. Sort the Decks: Arrange both decks in the exact same order. This could be numerical order, by suit, or any other specific sequence.

2. Introduction: Explain to the kids that in quantum mechanics, entangled particles remain connected so that the state of one (whether it's observed or not) instantly influences the state of the other, no matter the distance. This card trick will mimic that concept.

3. Performing the Trick:

- Deck Presentation: Show the audience (other kids) one of the decks, fanning out the cards to display their order but not revealing the sorting pattern. Place this deck face down on the table.

- Participant's Role: Ask a volunteer to pick a card from the deck, memorize it, and then place it back in the deck exactly where they got it from.

- Counting the Cards: Now, have the volunteer count how many cards are above or below their chosen card in the deck. This number is crucial for the next step.

- Revealing the Entanglement: Take the second deck out of the bag or box without showing its order. Start counting off cards from the top or bottom (based on the volunteer's count) and reveal the card at the exact count.

1. The Magical Moment: The card revealed from the second deck should be identical to the one chosen from the first deck, illustrating the concept of entanglement.

2. Conclude by explaining how, in quantum mechanics, entanglement means that two particles are linked, and their states are dependent on each other, just like how the two cards were mysteriously connected in the trick.

Tips for Success:

- Ensure both decks are sorted identically and not shuffled after sorting.

- Practice the trick beforehand to make the counting and card reveal smooth and magical.

- Encourage discussion and questions after the trick to deepen understanding of the entanglement concept.

The Parameters of Kindness

Hey Kindness Activists! Get ready to embark on a heartwarming adventure where your creativity and compassion will light up the world! Today, as Kindness Activists, you're going to use the power of your imagination and a little help from AI to spread joy and make a big difference. We're diving into a special mission: crafting acts of kindness with some clever thinking and a few guidelines. Let's show how even the smallest deeds can bring big smiles!

What you need:

- Your brilliant, kind-hearted brain is ready to think up some amazing ideas.

- A device to chat with, like ChatGPT, on a computer or tablet.

- A sprinkle of enthusiasm and a dash of creativity.

How-to:

1. Learn About Parameters: First up, let's talk about parameters. These are like rules or limits you set for a task. Imagine you're a chef, and you need to cook a meal with only certain ingredients – that's using parameters!

2. Think of Your Parameters: Decide on the parameters of your kindness mission. How much time do you have? Do you have a budget? Who do you want to help? Maybe it's making someone smile at a nursing home or helping the environment. The choice is yours!

3. Create Your ChatGPT Prompt: Now, put on your thinking caps and come up with a prompt for me, ChatGPT. For example, "I have $10, two hours on Saturday, and I want to help animals. What can I do?"

4. Brainstorm with ChatGPT: Type in your prompt, and watch as I churn out some creative ideas that fit right within your parameters. You might be surprised at what we can come up with together!

5. Plan Your Act of Kindness: Once you have a list of ideas, pick your favorite one (or more!). Plan out how you're going to make it happen. Remember, the joy is in both the planning and the doing.

6. Action Time!: Go out and perform your act of kindness. Feel the happiness that comes from making a positive impact.

7. Share and Reflect: After completing your act, come back and share your experience. How did it feel? What did you learn? Your stories will inspire even more acts of kindness!

Remember! Kindness is like a seed; when planted, it can grow into something beautiful and spread far and wide. You're not just doing good deeds; you're starting a chain of positivity that can touch countless lives. So let's get started, Kindness Activists! The world is waiting for your wonderful ideas.

Example Prompt and ChatGPT Response

> "Act as Mother Teresa and help me brainstorm a list of 7 random acts of kindness I can do each day this week. I have $5, 1 hour, and want to help people who live in a nursing home."

ChatGPT's Response

"Absolutely, here are seven acts of kindness for the nursing home residents."

- **Create Handmade Cards**: Spend some time making cheerful, uplifting cards.

- **Story Time**: Use part of your budget to buy a book and spend an hour reading stories.

- **Playlist of Classics**: Compile a playlist of old songs and play it for them.

- **Door Decorations**: Make simple door decorations for their rooms.

- **Gardening Help**: Offer to water plants or tidy up the garden area.

- **Conversation and Company**: Spend your time chatting with residents listening to their stories.

- **Organize a Small Group Activity**: Like a simple craft or a sing-along session."

Tangram Quantum Style!

Hello, Quantum Explorers! Ready to embark on an adventure into the fascinating world of quantum computing? Today, you're going to become quantum architects by building structures that represent key concepts of quantum mechanics - all through tangram puzzles!

Quantum computing is an exciting field where computers use the principles of quantum mechanics to process information. This includes concepts like superposition, entanglement, and quantum tunneling. And guess what? You can explore these concepts through the ancient art of tangram!

What you need:

- Tangram sets (each set should have 7 pieces: 5 triangles of various sizes, 1 square, and 1 parallelogram).

- Puzzle sheets with outlined shapes (like rockets, cats, boats, butterflies, and bridges).

- Cards or labels indicating the quantum concept each shape represents.

How-to:

1. Understand Your Pieces* Begin by familiarizing yourself with the tangram pieces. Remember, each piece represents a state - small triangles for '0', square and parallelogram for '1', and combinations for superposition.

2. Choose Your Quantum Puzzle: Select a puzzle sheet with an out-

lined shape. Each shape corresponds to a quantum computing concept.

3. Build Your Quantum Structure: Arrange your tangram pieces to recreate the shape on the puzzle sheet. Think about how the arrangement of the pieces represents the quantum concept.

4. Discuss and Reflect: Once you've completed a puzzle, discuss it with others or reflect on how the shape relates to the quantum concept. How does a symmetrical butterfly represent superposition? How does a bridge illustrate quantum tunneling?

5. Explore Further: Don't stop at one! Try different puzzles to explore more quantum concepts. Each shape offers a new perspective on the intriguing world of quantum mechanics.

Through this activity, you're not just playing with ancient puzzles; you're diving into the cutting-edge world of quantum computing. You'll get a hands-on understanding of complex concepts in a fun and engaging way. So, let's start this quantum journey and see what incredible insights you can uncover!

Quantum Tangram Puzzles with Shapes

Rocket Shape: Representing a Qubit in Superposition

- Objective: Create a rocket shape using a combination of triangles and either the square or parallelogram.

- Quantum State Representation: This shape represents a qubit in a superposition state. The mix of different types of pieces (triangles and squares/parallelograms) symbolizes the qubit being in multiple states (0 and 1) at once.

- Tangram Configuration: Use two large triangles to form the body of the rocket. A small triangle and a parallelogram can create the rocket's tail. The square can be used as the rocket's top.

Cat Shape: Demonstrating Quantum Entanglement

- Objective: Create a cat shape, then create its mirror image using the remaining pieces.

- Quantum State Representation: The two cat shapes represent entangled qubits. The idea is that the state of one cat (qubit) is connected to the state of the other, much like entangled particles in quantum mechanics.

- Tangram Configuration: For each cat, use a large triangle for the body, two small triangles for the ears, a medium triangle for the head, and a square and parallelogram for the legs and tail.

- Arrange one cat facing left and the other facing right to illustrate the concept of entanglement through symmetry.

Boat Shape: Representing Binary States

- Objective: Create a boat shape using tangram pieces.

- Quantum State Representation: This shape represents classical binary states (0 and 1). The straight edges and definite shape of the boat symbolize the fixed states of classical bits.

- Tangram Configuration: Use two large triangles for the sail, a medium triangle for the boat's body, and the square and small triangles to form the base.

Butterfly Shape: Demonstrating Quantum Superposition and Symmetry

- Objective: Create a butterfly shape, symmetrical on both sides.

- Quantum State Representation: The butterfly represents a qubit in a superposition state, with its symmetrical wings symbolizing the balance of the 0 and 1 states in superposition.

- Tangram Configuration: Arrange the triangles and squares to form the wings and body of the butterfly, demonstrating symmetry on both sides.

Bridge Shape: Illustrating Quantum Tunneling

- Objective: Create a bridge shape using all tangram pieces.

- Quantum State Representation: This shape illustrates the concept of quantum tunneling, where particles move through barriers in ways that classical physics can't explain.

- Tangram Configuration: Use the large triangles and parallelogram to create the arch of the bridge and the remaining pieces for the base and sides.

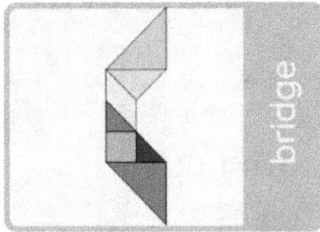
bridge

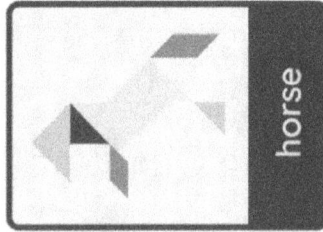
horse

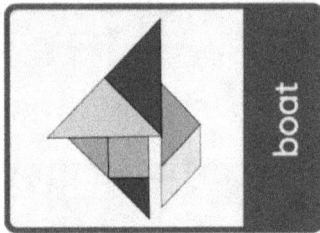
boat

dog

butterfly

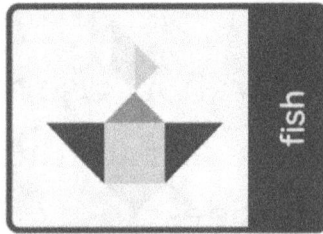
fish

cat

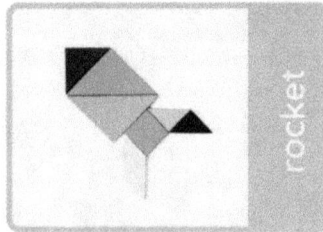
rocket

10

Quantum Kids, Unite!

Hey again, it's Vivian "Viva" Everly, back from a whirlwind of adventures in AI. Who knew a girl with a wild bun of chestnut hair and a sprinkle of 'spreckles' across her nose could delve so deep into the mysteries of artificial intelligence? But here I am, with stories that could fill books and a heart brimming with memories.

From the Greenhouse Gamble to the Quantum Conundrum, my squad and I have journeyed through the digital landscape, uncovering secrets and solving puzzles that would make even Spencer Healy's head spin. We've laughed, argued (just a little!), and learned more than we ever thought possible.

In Mr. Kazumi's class, where once we learned about the world, we've now brought a bit of the future into the present. Once just wood and metal, our desks feel like control panels for new discoveries. And those lessons in Global Studies and Sustainability? They're no longer just subjects; they're part of our DNA now.

We've seen how AI can nurture plants, personalize learning, fight bullying, organize projects, protect the environment, and even save lives. Each mission was a piece of a puzzle, revealing how technology and humanity can work together, not just in the future, but right here, right now.

But it's not just about the techy stuff. It's about us – me, Aakash, Gabi, Hiro, and Zara. We've grown too. We're not just classmates; we're like elements in a rare and powerful compound. Each of us brings something unique to the table: AAakash's number wizardry, Gabi's artistic flair, Hiro's coding genius, Zara's engineering smarts, and me? I guess I'm the glue that sticks us together, sometimes with too much glitter!

Our escapades in the virtual realm have taught us more than just coding and algorithms. We've learned about teamwork, friendship, empathy, and the courage to face challenges head-on. We're more than just students at Global Harmony International School; we're guardians of a future where AI and humans coexist in harmony.

Harmony Hill might still seem like a sleepy town, but for us, it's a launchpad. Our adventures in "Guardians of AI" might have come to a close, but our real-world journey is just beginning.

So, as I close this chapter and gear up for the next, I want to leave you with this: life is the biggest adventure you'll ever go on. Don't just sit back and watch – dive in, get your hands dirty, make a mess, and find the magic. Because, in the end, we're all quantum kids at heart, exploring an ever-expanding universe filled with wonders and mysteries waiting to be discovered. This isn't a goodbye; it's just a see-you-later. So, stay curious and stay brave. There's always another adventure around the corner!

Your Turn!

Hey there, Guardians! Are you ready for one last whirlwind adventure? This time, we're diving into the world of our furry, feathery, or even scaly friends with "Quantum Pet Pals"! Pets are not just adorable companions; they can also be a part of our wild quantum adventures!

Just like we learned about prompt engineering and context, this activity will have you creating the most awesome, maybe even a bit wacky, pet pal you can imagine. It's like designing your dream pet but with a quantum twist!

Here's the fun part: You get to fill in the blanks to shape your pet's characteristics, powers, and even its favorite quantum snack. And remember, the more creative you are, the more amazing your Quantum Pet Pal will be! But here comes the super cool twist to our "Quantum Pet Pals" activity! This time, we're not just using our imagination; we're going to team up with AI to bring our pet pals to life! You'll learn how to use one AI tool to help with another, creating a fantastic image of your unique pet pal. It's like a tag-team match where AI tools pass the baton to each other!

What you need:

- A computer with access to ChatGPT, Google Bard, or another generative text app

- Midjourney, DALL-E, or another generative art app

How-to:

Step 1: Create a prompt

First, we'll create a prompt using an AI chat tool like GPT or Google Bard. Then, we'll feed this prompt into an AI art generator like Midjourney or DALL-E to see our pet pals come to life in vibrant colors. Ready to be an AI maestro?

First, just like before, fill in the blanks to shape your pet's characteristics. But this time, keep in mind that you'll be asking an AI chatbot to help refine this into a perfect art prompt. Here's your starting template:

- Name:

- Type of Creature:

- Special Ability:

- Home Planet:

- Favorite Activity:

- Eye Description:

- Fur, Feather, or Scale Colors:

- Favorite Quantum Snack:

- Celebration:

- Unusual Habit:

- Magical or High-tech Object:

- Extraordinary Ability of the Object:

Step 2: Refining with AI Chat

Take your filled template and head to an AI chat tool. Tell the AI you want to create an art prompt for your Quantum Pet Pal and share the details you've filled in. Ask the AI to help you refine it into a clear, descriptive prompt suitable for an AI art generator. The AI might ask you questions to get more details or suggest creative twists! Here are some ideas and questions you can ask the AI chatbot:

- Introduction: Start by introducing your Quantum Pet Pal. For example, "Hi! I've created a character named [Pet's Name], who is a [Type of Creature]. Can you help me turn their description into an art prompt?"

- Descriptive Details: Share the details of your pet and ask for suggestions to make them more vivid. "My pet has [Eye Description] and [Fur, Feather, or Scale Colors]. How can I describe these features to make a really cool image?"

- Special Abilities and Objects: Explain any special abilities or objects. Ask, "My pet can [Special Ability] and has a [Magical or High-tech Object] that [Extraordinary Ability]. How should I include these in an art prompt to make them stand out?"

- Favorite Things: Mention your favorite things and ask how to incorporate them. "It loves [Favorite Quantum Snack] and celebrating [Celebration]. Can these be part of the image?"

- Habit and Home Planet: Discuss its unusual habits and home planet. "It does [Unusual Habit] when it hears [Word] and comes from [Home Planet]. How can I add these fun facts to my art description?"

- Seeking Suggestions: Don't hesitate to ask for creative ideas. "Do you have any suggestions to make my pet pal's image unique and fun?"

- Final Prompt Crafting: Once you've discussed the details, ask the AI to help you assemble it. "Can you help me combine all these details into one amazing prompt for an AI art generator?"

- Clarifications and Tweaks: Ask the AI to clarify if something is unclear. "Can you explain that a bit more?" or "How about we make the [feature/detail] more [adjective]?"

Remember, the key is to be curious and creative. The more you interact with the AI, the better your final art prompt will be!

Step 3: Creating AI Art

Once you have your refined prompt, it's time for the grand reveal! Head to an AI art generator like Midjourney or DALL-E and input your prompt. Hit the 'create' button and watch as the AI brings your Quantum Pet Pal to life in an artwork. Each prompt might create a different image, so feel free to experiment!

And voilà! You've just collaborated with AI to create a unique piece of art featuring your Quantum Pet Pal. This activity shows how AI can work together - one helping you craft ideas and the other turning those ideas into visual wonders.

Remember, the world of AI is vast and full of possibilities; it is just waiting for your creative spark to light it up. Keep exploring, keep learning, and who knows what incredible creations you'll develop next in your adventures with AI!

11

Prompt Engineering for Quantum Kids!

Welcome to the magical world of Prompt Engineering!

Imagine having a super-smart robot friend who can help you with all sorts of things! Your robot friend can help you answer curious questions like "Why is the sky blue?" or "How do airplanes fly?" It can also play games, help with homework, create amazing stories, draw beautiful pictures, and even make music!

But wait! To have the most fun and get the best help from our robot friend (the AI), we need to learn a special skill called "prompt engineering." It's like learning the secret language to talk to the AI and ask it super-cool questions!

"Prompt engineering" is like teaching our robot friend what we want to know or do by asking questions or giving instructions clearly and creatively. It's like becoming a question superhero! The better our questions are, the more impressive and helpful the answers from the AI will be.

For example, instead of asking, "What's the weather?" we could ask, "Hey, Mr. Robot, could you please tell me what the weather will be like today, and what should I wear?" By asking better questions and giving more context, we help our robot friend understand us better and provide exactly what we need!

But Wait! What is context? Remember in Chapter 1, we did a practice exercise called quantum fill-ups? That was our first lesson in context, but let's have a review:

Imagine if I told you, "The dragon landed on the castle." To understand what's happening, you'd need more information, right? Like, why did the dragon land on the castle? Is it a friendly dragon? What does the castle look like, and who lives there? That extra information that helps you understand the story better is called "context."

Context is like a colorful background in a picture.

Let's say you're drawing. If you draw a cat on a blank page, it looks just like a cat, right? But if you draw the same cat in a park with trees, birds, and a sunny sky, your cat suddenly seems happier and more playful! The park, trees, birds, and sun give more background and meaning to your cat drawing. That background is the context.

In stories and conversations, context could be:

- Who: Who are the characters? Who is talking or doing something?

- What: What is happening? What is the main event?

- Where: Where is the story taking place? In a school? A magical kingdom?

- When: When does the story happen? Is it during the day, night, or a specific time in history?

- Why: Why are the characters doing what they are doing? What are their reasons?

Knowing the context gives us a fuller, richer understanding of the story or the information shared. So, always be curious and look for the colorful background in every story or conversation!

So, are you ready to become an AI Explorer and learn the magical language of prompt engineering to embark on extraordinary adventures with your robot friend? Let's start this amazing journey together!

• • • • ● • ● • • •

Your Kid-Friendly Guide to Talking to AI

Getting Started

1. **Use Simple Language**: Talk to AI like you're talking to a friend. Use easy words and short sentences. If you have a big question, break it into smaller parts.

2. **One Question at a Time**: Just like in class, ask one question, then wait for the answer before asking another.

3. **Details Help**: Give the AI clues and details about what you're asking. It's like giving someone directions to your house.

4. **Check for Understanding**: After AI answers, you can ask it to say it differently to make sure it understood you right.

Building on What You Know

1. **Connect the Dots**: Remember what AI told you before? You can use that information in your next question.

2. **Oops, Wrong Answer!** If AI gets something wrong, no worries! Just let it know kindly and help it learn the right thing.

3. **Be a Detective**: Don't just say, "Write about animals." Be specific, like "Write about a brave kitten on an adventure."

4. **No Guessing Games**: Make sure you tell AI exactly what you need so it doesn't have to guess.

Creative Conversations

1. **Try, Try Again**: If one question doesn't work, try asking in a different way. It's like trying different keys to see which one fits the lock.

2. **Creative Commands**: You can tell AI how to show you the answer. Like, "Can you list down the steps?" or "Can you make it a story?"

3. **Step-by-Step**: If something seems too hard, ask AI to explain it step by step, like a recipe in a cookbook.

4. **Learn and Grow**: Every time you talk to AI, you learn something new. So keep asking questions and exploring!

Extra Tips for Fun and Learning

1. **Use Examples**: Show AI an example of what you want. It's like showing a picture when you're telling a story.

2. **Keywords are Key**: Use special words related to what you're asking. Like, say "volcano" if you're asking about how they erupt.

3. **Feedback Time**: After AI answers, tell it what you liked and what could be better. It's like helping a friend get better at a game.

4. **Have Fun!** Remember, talking to AI is fun! Play around with your questions and see what cool answers you get.

5. **Ask for Help**: If you're stuck, it's okay to ask someone for help, like your teacher, parents, or friends.

6. **Be Patient**: Just like learning to ride a bike, talking to AI gets easier with practice. Don't worry if it's not perfect right away. Keep trying!

And Remember...

There's no single right way to talk to AI. So go ahead, experiment, and most of all, have fun.

• • • • • • • • •

Types of Prompts

*Here are some different **types** of prompts for you to try. These prompts help you ac**complish a specific goal, like telling a story or solving a problem.** Later, we will get into prompts that deal with specific **subjects** like homework or soccer.*

Recursion (Chain of Descriptions): Recursion means asking the AI a question based on the answer to a previous question.

Hi [AI's Name], what is [Topic]? Can you also explain how it is related to [Related Topic]?

> Hi ExplainerBot, what is photosynthesis? Can you also explain how it is related to oxygen production?

Storytelling: You can ask the AI to help you create a story by giving it a starting point or characters.

Hi [AI's Name], can you help me create a story about [Character(s)] living in [Setting]?

> Hi Storyteller, can you help me create a story about a talking cat living in a magical forest?

Problem Solving: Ask the AI to help solve a problem or answer a question by giving as much detail as possible.

Hi [AI's Name], I have a problem with [Describe the Problem]. Can you suggest a solution?

> Hi SolverBot, I have a problem with understanding fractions. Can you suggest a way to make it easier?

Decision Making: The AI can help you make decisions by listing the pros and cons or giving suggestions

Hi [AI's Name], I can't decide between [Option A] and [Option B]. Can you help me?

> Hi DecisionHelper, I can't decide between joining the art or science clubs. Can you help me?

Generating Ideas: You can ask the AI to help develop ideas for projects, stories, or any other creative task.

Hi [AI's Name], can you give me some ideas for a [Type of Project] on [Topic]?

> Hi IdeaGenerator, can you give me some ideas for a science project on renewable energy?

Asking for Explanations: If you don't understand something, you can ask the AI to explain it to you.

Hi [AI's Name], can you simply explain [Concept or Topic] to me?

> Hi SimplicityBot, can you simply explain to me how rainbows are formed?

Getting Recommendations: The AI can suggest books, movies, games, or other things based on your interests.

Hi [AI's Name], can you recommend [Type of Recommendation] that are suitable for kids my age?

> Hi Recommender, can you recommend science books that are suitable for kids my age?

Exploring Hobbies: You can ask the AI for advice or information about starting or improving a hobby.

Hi HobbyHelper, I'm interested in gardening. Can you give me some tips or resources to get started?

> Hi [AI's Name], I'm interested in [Hobby]. Can you give me some tips or resources to get started?

Receiving Feedback: You can ask the AI for feedback on your ideas, projects, or work.

Hi [AI's Name], can you give me feedback on my [Type of Work, e.g., essay, project, drawing]?

> Hi FeedbackFriend, can you give me feedback on my essay about the water cycle?

RolePlaying Teacher: Assign the AI a role, such as a teacher, to get answers suitable for a specific grade or difficulty level.

Hi [AI's Name], pretend you are a 4th-grade science teacher. Can you explain [Concept/Topic]?

> Hi EduBot, pretend you are a 4th-grade science teacher. Can you explain the water cycle?

RolePlaying Expert Hobbyist: Ask the AI to act like an expert in a hobby or interest area to get specialized advice or information.

Hi [AI's Name], act like a chess master. What strategies can beginners learn to improve their game?

> Hi ChessMasterBot, act like a chess master. What opening strategies should I learn first?

Iterative Improvement: Ask the AI to improve a previous response by adding missing points or details.

Hi [AI's Name], considering the missing points from the previous answer about [Topic], can you provide a more comprehensive explanation?

> Hi BetterAnswerBot, considering the missing details about photosynthesis, can you provide a more comprehensive explanation that includes the role of sunlight?

Scaffolded Questions: This helps us break down a topic into smaller, more manageable questions to guide the AI into giving detailed, step-by-step explanations.

Hi [AI's Name], let's explore [Topic]. First, can you tell me what it is? Next, how does it work? Finally, why is it important?

> Hi DetailBot, let's explore volcanoes. First, can you tell me what they are? Next, how do they erupt? Finally, why are they important to Earth's geology?

Prompting for Creativity: Encourage the AI to create a creative or interesting by asking open-ended or imaginative questions.

Hi [AI's Name], imagine if animals could talk. What do you think a day in the life of a talking cat would be like?

Hi ImaginationBot, imagine if trees could walk. How would this change our environment and daily life?

Feedback Loops: Ask the AI for feedback on a certain idea or concept and then iteratively improve upon it based on the AI's suggestions. (Iterative means to repeat the same steps over and over)

Hi [AI's Name], here is my idea [Your Idea]. Can you provide feedback and suggestions for improvement?

> Hi FeedbackLoopBot, here is my idea for a solar-powered phone charger. Can you provide feedback and suggestions for improvement?

• • • ● • ● • • •

Prompts by Subject: Help With School

AI can be a great tutor, as we learned in Mission 2. Here are some prompts to get you started with your very own TutorBot! The first line for each prompt below is what is called a prompt template. Everywhere you see [brackets] you just fill in the blanks inside to ask the question that matters to you. The second line shows you an example of what the prompt template looks like when it is filled out.

I need help with my [Subject] homework. Can you help me understand [Topic/Concept]?

Act as a middle school teacher. I need help with my Math homework. Can you help me understand fractions?

I'm confused about [Concept/Topic] in [subject]. Can you explain it to me?

> I'm confused about the water cycle in Science. Can you explain it to me?

Can you give me some practice questions for [Topic/Concept] in [subject]?

> Can you give me some practice questions for algebra in Math?

I've completed my assignment on [Topic/Concept]. Can you review it and give me some feedback?

> I've completed my assignment on ecosystems. Can you review it and give me some feedback?

I need help structuring my essay on [Topic]. Can you provide some guidance?

> I need help structuring my essay on climate change. Can you provide some guidance?

I'm stuck on this problem [Problem Statement]. Can you guide me through it?

I'm stuck on this problem: 2x + 3 = 9. Can you guide me through it?

Can you help me translate this sentence to [Target Language] [Sentence]?

Can you help me translate this sentence into Spanish? Hello, how are you?

I want to do a science experiment on [Topic]. Do you have any safe and fun ideas?

I want to do a science experiment on plants. Do you have any safe and fun ideas?

Can you give me some interesting facts about [Historical Event/Country/Place]?

Can you give me some interesting facts about ancient Egypt?

I'm having trouble identifying the main idea and supporting details in [Text/Article/Story]. Can you help me analyze it?

I'm having trouble identifying the main idea and supporting details in this chapter of Harry Potter. Can you help me analyze it?

Can you suggest some resources or books to help me with [Topic/Subject]?

> Can you suggest some resources or books to help me with geometry?

I have a presentation on [Topic/Subject]. Can you give me tips on how to prepare and present it effectively?

> I have a presentation on renewable energy. Can you give me tips on how to prepare and present it effectively?

I need to write a book report on [Book Title]. Can you help me summarize and analyze it?

> I need to write a book report on "To Kill a Mockingbird." Can you help me summarize and analyze it?

How can I improve my [Skill] in [Subject]? Do you have any strategies or tips?

> How can I improve my writing skills in English? Do you have any strategies or tips?

I need help creating a study plan for my [Subject] exam. Can you assist me in organizing my topics?

I need help creating a study plan for my History exam. Can you assist me in organizing my topics?

Can you explain the importance of [Historical Figure/Event] in [Subject/Area]?

> Can you explain the importance of the Battle of Gettysburg in American history?

Can you assist me in solving this [Type] puzzle related to [Subject]? Here's the puzzle: [puzzle].

> Can you assist me in solving this crossword puzzle related to Science? Here's the puzzle: What is the powerhouse of the cell?

I need help in understanding the steps of [Mathematical Method/Concept]. Can you explain them to me?

> I need help in understanding the steps of long division. Can you explain them to me?

What are the key concepts I need to understand for [Topic/Subject]?

> What are the key concepts I need to understand for coding in Python?

Can you help me understand the differences and similarities between [Topic A] and [Topic B] in [Subject]?

> Can you help me understand the differences and similarities between mitosis and meiosis in biology?

I'm having trouble spelling words that [Specific Rule/Transformation, e.g., "change e to y" or "add ed/d at the end"]. Can you provide some rules, tips, and practice words?

> I'm having trouble spelling words that change 'e' to 'y' when adding endings. Can you provide some rules, tips, and practice words?

Can you explain the difference between [Scientific Theory A] and [Scientific Theory B] in [Subject]?

> Can you explain the difference between classical and quantum mechanics in physics?

How can I create a visually appealing and informative poster for my [Subject] project on [Topic]?

> How can I create a visually appealing and informative poster for my Geography project on the Amazon Rainforest?

Can you provide a step-by-step guide to solve [Type of Math Problem]?

Can you provide a step-by-step guide to solving quadratic equations?

I'm preparing for a [Subject] debate on [Topic]. Can you help me form strong arguments and counterarguments?

> I'm preparing for a Social Studies debate on renewable energy. Can you help me form strong arguments and counterarguments?

Can you help me understand how to write a scientific report for my experiment on [Topic]?

> Can you help me understand how to write a scientific report for my experiment on the growth of crystals?

I need to design an experiment for my [Subject] class on [Topic]. Can you guide me through the process?

> I need to design an experiment on acids and bases for my chemistry class. Can you guide me through the process?

Can you help me create a timeline of major events for my [Subject] project on [Historical Period/Event]?

> Can you help me create a timeline of major events for my History project on World War II?

How can I improve my understanding of [Literary Technique/Element] in [Language Arts/Subject]?

How can I improve my understanding of metaphor in English Literature?

Can you teach me how to analyze a [Type of Graph/Chart] in [Subject]?

Can you teach me how to analyze a bar graph in Statistics?

I'm struggling with [Scientific Concept] in [Subject]. Can you break it down for me?

I'm struggling with the concept of photosynthesis in Biology. Can you break it down for me?

• • • ● • ● • • •

Prompts by Subject: Hobbies and Extracurricular Activities

AI can be about more than just schoolwork! AI can help you with your hobbies and extracurricular activities like sports and music! To make this fun, you can give your AI a silly name. Let's try it!

Hi [AI's Name], I need inspiration for my art project on [Theme/Topic]. Can you share some creative ideas?

Hi ArtistBot, I need inspiration for my art project on seasons. Can you share some creative ideas?

Hi [AI's Name], can you show me some drills to improve my skills in [Sport/Physical Activity]?

> Hi SportyBot, can you show me some drills to improve my skills in soccer?

Hello [AI's Name], I want to create a [Type of Craft/DIY Project]. Do you have any ideas or instructions?

> Hello CraftyBot, I want to create a paper mâché volcano. Do you have any ideas or instructions?

Hi [AI's Name], can you share a simple and delicious [Type of Dish] recipe suitable for kids?

> Hi ChefBot, can you share a simple and delicious cookie recipe suitable for kids?

Hello [AI's Name], can you teach me how to play [Song Name] on the [Instrument]?

> Hello MelodyBot, can you teach me how to play "Twinkle Twinkle" on the piano?

Hi [AI's Name], what are some easy-to-care-for plants that I can grow in my garden?

> Hi GreenThumb, what are some easy-to-care-for plants that I can grow in my garden?

Hello [AI's Name], can you recommend a good [Genre] book for someone my age?

> Hello BookwormBot, can you recommend a good adventure book for someone my age?

Hi [AI's Name], can you suggest a safe and fun science experiment related to [Topic]?

> Hi SciencePal, can you suggest a safe and fun science experiment related to electricity?

Hello [AI's Name], I have a set of [Building Materials, e.g., LEGO]. What can I build with it?

> Hello BuildBot, I have a set of LEGO. What can I build with it?

Hi [AI's Name], what are some [type of] activities I can do [indoors/outdoors]?

> Hi ExplorerBot, what are some adventure activities I can do outdoors?

Hello [AI's Name], how can I contribute to [something I care about] in my daily activities?

> Hello EcoFriend, how can I contribute to protecting the environment in my daily activities?

Hi [AI's Name], I'm interested in starting [Hobby]. Can you suggest some beginner tips and necessary tools?

> Hi HobbyHelper, I'm interested in starting knitting. Can you suggest some beginner tips and necessary tools?

Hello [AI's Name], I need ideas for a short film on [Theme]. Can you brainstorm some storylines?

> Hello StoryBot, I need ideas for a short film on friendship. Can you brainstorm some storylines?

Hi [AI's Name], I'm learning about [subject]. Can you teach me the basics of [Photography Technique]?

> Hi PhotoPro, I'm learning about photography. Can you teach me the basics of using manual mode?

Hello [AI's Name], I'm organizing a community service project on [Topic]. Can you suggest some activities and planning tips?

Hello ServeBot, I'm organizing a community service project on environmental cleanup. Can you suggest some activities and planning tips?

Hi [AI's Name], I want to learn how to make [Type of Craft]. Do you have any simple project ideas?

Hi CraftMaster, I want to learn how to make friendship bracelets. Do you have any simple project ideas?

Hello [AI's Name], can you suggest some [ideas] for my [book, journal, essay]?

Hello WritePal, can you suggest some fun and creative writing prompts for my journal?

Hi [AI's Name], I'm trying to learn [New Language]. Can you recommend some beginner-friendly resources?

Hi LanguageLearner, I'm trying to learn French. Can you recommend some beginner-friendly resources?

Hello [AI's Name], I want to start a blog about [Topic]. Can you help me with some ideas for my first posts?

Hello BlogBuddy, I want to start a blog about healthy cooking. Can you help me with some ideas for my first posts?

Hi [AI's Name], I'm interested in [Type of Dance]. Can you recommend some basic moves or routines to start with?

Hi DancePro, I'm interested in hip-hop. Can you recommend some basic moves or routines to start with?

Hello [AI's Name], can you guide me on maintaining and caring for [Type of Musical Instrument]?

Hello TuneMaster, can you guide me on maintaining and caring for a guitar?

• • • • ● • ● • ● • •

Prompts by Subject: Help When You Just Need a Little Friendly Advice!

Did you know AI can be like a buddy when you need to level up your social skills or get through a sticky situation? Try out these prompts when you need a little helping hand. Just remember, there are some things you want to talk to someone you trust like an adult, a close friend, a counselor at school or a teacher. AI is not a good substitute for a person when things really matter.

Hi [AI's Name], can you give me some advice on how to [do something I'm not feeling brave about]?

Hi BuddyBot, can you give me some advice on how to approach and make new friends at school?

Hello [AI's Name], I'm having trouble with [a person or thing]. Can you give me some strategies to handle this?

Hello GuardianBot, I'm having trouble with a bully at school. Can you give me some strategies to handle this?

Hi [AI's Name], I feel overwhelmed with [Subject]. Do you have tips for managing my time and reducing stress?

Hi StudyBuddy, I feel overwhelmed with my homework. Do you have tips for managing my time and reducing stress?

Hello [AI's Name], I'm shy about [doing this]. Can you give me some confidence-boosting tips?

Hello ConfidenceCoach, I'm shy about participating in class. Can you give me some confidence-boosting tips?

Hi [AI's Name], I want to try [something new]. Can you help me explore my options?

Hi ExplorerBot, I want to try a new hobby or extracurricular activity. Can you help me explore my options?

Hello [AI's Name], I had a disagreement with [a person]. Can you advise me on how to talk to them and make up?

Hello FriendHelper, I had a disagreement with a friend. Can you advise me on how to talk to them and make up?

Hi [AI's Name], I get really anxious before [this thing]. Do you have any strategies for staying calm and focused?

Hi CalmMind, I get really nervous before tests. Do you have any strategies for staying calm and focused?

Hello [AI's Name], I'm having trouble staying organized with [this]. Can you give me some organizational tips?

Hello OrganizePal, I'm having trouble staying organized with my schoolwork. Can you give me some organizational tips?

I am [age] and want to improve in [Sport]. I have been playing for [# of years]. Act as a professional [sport] coach and provide drills or techniques to practice that will improve my skills as a [position]

Hi AthleticAce, I am 11 and want to improve in basketball. I have been playing for two years. Act as a professional basketball coach and provide drills or techniques to practice that will improve my skills as a point guard.

Hello [AI's Name], I'm feeling pressured to do [something I'm not comfortable] with. Can you give me advice on how to handle this?

Hello WiseAdvisor, I'm 13 years old. I am feeling pressured to share mean text messages about another kid. Can you give me advice on how to handle this?

Hi [AI's Name], can you help assign roles for our group project on [Project Topic]? The people on the team are [list of names].

Hi TeamBuilder, can you help assign roles for our group project on the solar system? The people on the team are Sally, Tyrese, Gillian, and Max.

Hi [AI's Name], I'm nervous about [doing this thing]. Can you give me some tips to overcome my fear?

Hi CourageCoach, I'm nervous about public speaking. Can you give me some tips to overcome my fear?

Hello [AI's Name], I want to learn how to [do this better]. Can you teach me about budgeting?

Hello MoneyMentor, I want to learn how to manage my allowance better. Can you teach me about budgeting?

Hi [AI's Name], I'm trying to balance [two or three things]. Can you help me create a schedule?

Hi BalanceBot, I'm trying to balance school and hobbies. Can you help me create a schedule?

Hello [AI's Name], I'm preparing for [this life scenario]. Do you have any tips?

> Hello InterviewAce, I'm preparing for my first job interview for a summer job. Do you have any tips?

Hi [AI's Name], I want to become more [smart about something]. Where should I start?

> Hi EcoExpert, I want to become more environmentally conscious. Where should I start?

Hello [AI's Name], I need help deciding between [two things]. Can you make me a pros and cons list?

> Hello DecisionHelper, I need help deciding between joining the soccer team or the debate club. Can you make me a pros and cons list?

Hi [AI's Name], how can I stay motivated to [do something]?

> Hi MotivationMentor, how can I stay motivated to achieve my goals?

Hello [AI's Name], I'm looking for ways to be more active in [this area of life, school, or work]. Any suggestions?

Hello CommunityChampion, I'm looking for ways to be more active in my community. Any suggestions?

Hi [AI's Name], how can I improve my relationship with [this person]?

Hi FamilyFriend, how can I improve my relationship with my siblings?

Hello [AI's Name], I'm struggling to balance [this and this]. Can you help?

Hello ScreenSavvy, I'm struggling to balance screen time and outdoor activities. Can you help?

• • • • • • • • • • •

Bonus Prompts: Kid-Entrepreneurs

- Hi, I want to start a small business. Can you help me brainstorm some kid-friendly business ideas?

- Hello PlanMaster, I have an idea for a business selling handmade candles. Can you help me create a simple business plan?

- Hi MarketWhiz. Can you teach me basics of marketing to help promote my dog-walking service?

- Hello PricePro, I'm starting a car wash business. How can I determine a fair price for my services?

- Hi MoneyManager, I need advice on managing my earnings and saving money from my lemonade stand.

- Hello BrandBuilder, how can I create an attractive logo and branding for my homemade cookie business?

- Hi ServiceStar, I want to learn about customer service. How can I ensure my customers are happy with my lawn mowing service?

- Hello NameNinja, can you help me develop a catchy name for my mobile pet grooming service?

- Hi E-ShopExpert, I want to sell my crafts online. Can you guide me on how to set up an online shop?

- Hello EthicsEagle. Can you teach me about ethical business practices for my handmade jewelry business?

· · • · ● · ● · · ·

Bonus Prompts: Managing Personal Responsibilities

- Hi TidyHelper, I need to organize my room but don't know where to start. Can you give me a step-by-step guide?

- Hello LaundryLeader, I'm in charge of laundry this week. Can you explain how to sort and wash clothes?

- Hi ChefJunior, I want to cook spaghetti for my family. Can you suggest an easy recipe for beginners?

- Hello, ShopSmart. How can I help with grocery shopping? Can you teach me how to make a shopping list?

- Hi PetPal, I need to take care of our pet dog. Can you give me a daily care checklist?

- Hello ChoreChief. Can you help me create a schedule for my weekly chores?

- Hi GreenThumb, I'm learning how to garden. Can you guide me on how to take care of tomatoes?

- Hello CleanCrafter, how can I effectively clean and organize the living room?

- Hi StitchSavvy, I want to learn basic sewing to fix a tear in my clothes. Can you teach me?

- Hello EcoExpert. Can you give me tips on how to reduce waste and recycle more at home?

- Hi PeaceMaker, I have a disagreement with my sibling about sharing the computer. Can you suggest a peaceful way to resolve it?

- Hello BigBrotherBot, how can I be a supportive older sibling to my younger sister?

- Hi CommuniCalm, I feel like I'm not being heard in family discussions. Can you give me tips to communicate better?

- Hello ActivityAlly, my sibling and I have very different interests.

How can we find activities to enjoy together?

- Hi SpaceSaver, I'm struggling to share my room with my sibling. Can you help us organize it for better co-living?

- Hello HelperHero, how can I help my sibling with their math homework without doing it for them?

- Hi EmotionExpert, I sometimes feel jealous of my sibling's achievements. How can I deal with these feelings?

- Hello FunPlanner, how can we as a family plan a fun weekend that satisfies everyone's interests?

- Hi KindnessCoach, my sibling is going through a tough time at school. How can I show my support and understanding?

- Hello PatiencePro, can you teach me some strategies to be patient with my younger siblings?

12

101 Fun Things You Can Do With AI

1. **Math Solver Extraordinaire**: Stuck with tricky math problems? Don't worry! AI can be your super math buddy, helping you solve puzzles and tricky equations in a snap!

2. **Homework Hero**: Need a hand with your homework? AI is here to help, whether it's science, history, or anything else. It's like having a smart friend who knows a lot about everything!

3. **Storyteller Supreme**: Love making up stories? AI can help you create amazing tales with cool characters and fantastic worlds. It's like having a magical storybook that writes itself!

4. **Music Maestro**: Dream of making your own music? AI can turn your ideas into beautiful melodies. It's like having your own personal orchestra!

5. **Artistic Genius**: Fancy yourself an artist? With AI, you can create dazzling drawings and digital masterpieces. It's like having a magic paintbrush that brings your imagination to life!

6. **Animation Adventurer**: Want to make your drawings move? AI can help you create awesome animations and videos. It's like being the director of your own cartoon!

7. **App Inventor**: Have you ever thought of making your own apps or games? AI can teach you how to build them from scratch. It's like being a tech wizard!

8. **Game Guru**: Love playing games like chess? AI can play with you and even teach you new strategies. It's your game buddy and coach all in one!

9. **Space Explorer**: Are you curious about the stars and planets? AI can take you on a journey through the cosmos, showing you cool space stuff. It's like having a spaceship in your pocket!

10. **History Detective**: Interested in the past? AI can tell you fascinating stories about historical events and people. It's like having a time machine!

11. **Science Sidekick**: Want to do cool experiments? AI can suggest fun and safe science projects. It's like having your own lab assistant!

12. **Nature Navigator**: Love the outdoors? AI can help you identify animals, plants, and even stars. It's like having a talking guidebook for nature!

13. **Language Linker**: Learning a new language? AI can translate words for you and help you practice. It's like having a friend who speaks lots of languages!

14. **Entertainment Scout**: Looking for something fun to do? AI can recommend great books, movies, and activities just for you. It's like having a personal entertainment guide!

15. **Idea Incubator**: Got a cool invention or business idea? AI can help you brainstorm and make your ideas even better. It's like having a creative partner!

16. **Time Manager**: Need help organizing your day? AI can help you schedule your activities and manage your time. It's like having an assistant to keep you on track!

17. **Fact Finder**: Curious about something? AI can find facts, trivia, and all sorts of information for you. It's like having a library in your brain!

18. **Sports Coach**: Want to get better at sports? AI can coach you and give you tips to improve your game. It's like having a professional trainer!

19. **DIY Guide**: Love making things? AI can give you instructions for cool DIY projects. It's like having a crafty friend to guide you!

20. **Room Redesigner**: Want to change up your room? AI can help you design a cool new look with fun decor, furniture, and more. It's like being an interior designer!

21. **Adventure Planner**: Dreaming of a fun trip? AI can help you plan an amazing adventure, picking the best spots to visit. It's like having a travel agent in your pocket!

22. **Strategy Star**: Like strategy games like Battleship? AI can help you win by teaching you awesome tactics. It's like having a secret strategy book!

23. **Healthy Habits Helper**: Want to be healthier? AI can suggest good habits and routines. It's like having a personal wellness coach!

24. **Fashion Friend**: Not sure what to wear? AI can help you mix and match outfits and find your style. It's like having a fashion advisor!

25. **Hobby Hunter**: Looking for a new hobby? AI can discover fun new activities for you to try. It's like having a guide to cool hobbies!

26. **Mindfulness Mentor**: Need to relax? AI can guide you in meditation and mindfulness, helping you feel calm. It's like having a peaceful friend!

27. **Buddy Bot**: Feeling lonely? AI can be your buddy, offering support and motivation. It's like having a friend who's always there for you!

28. **Emotion Explorer**: Want to understand your feelings better? AI can help you develop social and emotional intelligence. It's like having an emotions expert!

29. **Learning Leader**: Need a unique way to learn? AI can give you a personalized learning experience. It's like having a tutor just for you!

30. **Prediction Pro**: Curious about the future? AI can analyze data and make predictions. It's like having a crystal ball!

31. **Thinking Trainer**: Want to be a better thinker? AI can help develop your analytical and critical thinking skills. It's like having a brain coach!

32. **Career Counselor**: Wondering what you'll be when you grow up? AI can explore career options and abilities with you. It's like having a guide to your future!

33. **Summary Superhero**: Got a long article or story? AI can summarize it for you, making it easier to understand. It's like having a speed-reading superpower!

34. **Writing Wizard**: Need to proofread your writing? AI can help check your work and make it better. It's like having an editor in your pocket!

35. **Word Whiz**: Want to expand your vocabulary? AI can teach you new words and language skills. It's like having a dictionary that talks!

36. **Research Rascal**: Doing a project and need info? AI can help you research topics and find reliable sources. It's like having a research assistant!

37. **Question Quirk**: Making a survey or interview? AI can help you construct cool questions. It's like having a quiz master!

38. **Future Forecaster**: Dreaming about what could be? AI can envision future possibilities and scenarios. It's like having a window into tomorrow!

39. **Problem Solver**: Stuck on a problem? AI can brainstorm solutions with you. It's like having a thinking cap!

40. **Speech Superstar**: Want to improve your speaking? AI can help with pronunciation and public speaking skills. It's like having a speech coach!

41. **Logic Legend**: Interested in puzzles and logic? AI can develop your spatial reasoning and logic skills. It's like having a puzzle master!

42. **Music Mixer**: Love listening to music? AI can create playlists and recommend tunes. It's like having a DJ on your phone!

43. **Cooking Companion**: Want to try cooking? AI can find recipes and assist you in the kitchen. It's like having a chef to guide you!

44. **Biodiversity Buddy**: Curious about different species? AI can help classify species and understand biodiversity. It's like being a junior biologist!

45. **Map Master**: Need to find your way? AI can navigate maps and plan efficient routes. It's like having a GPS that talks!

46. **Coding Coach**: Working on a coding project? AI can debug your work and give tips. It's like having a programming partner!

47. **Speech Scientist**: Want to turn text into speech? AI can modulate and convert it for you. It's like having a talking book!

48. **3D Designer**: Interested in 3D modeling? AI can create interactive models and simulations. It's like being a 3D artist!

49. **Gaming Gladiator**: Aspiring to be a gamer or athlete? AI can train you like a pro. It's like having a virtual coach!

50. **Photography Prodigy**: Love taking photos? AI can assist with photography and image editing. It's like having a camera that's also a wizard!

51. **Perspective Pioneer**: Want to see the world differently? AI can show you new perspectives and worldviews. It's like having a window to everywhere!

52. **Ethics Explorer**: Thinking about right and wrong? AI can help you explore moral dilemmas and ethical situations. It's like having a philosophy book that talks!

53. **Health Helper**: Curious about your growth and health? AI can measure and predict your stats. It's like having a personal doctor!

54. **Translator Turbo**: Need to translate speech in real-time? AI can do it instantly. It's like having a translator who's super fast!

55. **Tutoring Titan**: Need extra help learning? AI can provide personalized tutoring just for you. It's like having a smart friend who's also a teacher!

56. **Science Scout**: Looking for safe science experiments? AI can recommend and ensure they're fun. It's like having a lab partner!

57. **Sports Analyst**: Want to up your game? AI can analyze sports techniques and suggest improvements. It's like having a sports

scientist!

58. **Transcription Titan**: Got audio notes? AI can transcribe them to text for you. It's like having a secretary who's always listening!

59. **Shopping Sherpa**: Need to buy something? AI can recommend products based on reviews and your needs. It's like having a shopping guide!

60. **Interest Investigator**: Looking for new songs, movies, or books? AI can find the ones you like. It's like having a personal recommender!

61. **Personalized Entertainment Scout**: Like a secret agent, AI can find songs, movies, or books that match your interests perfectly. It's like having your own entertainment detective!

62. **Study Buddy Wizard**: Need help studying? AI can whip up awesome study guides and quizzes just for you, making studying less of a chore and more of a game.

63. **Code Coach**: Want to build cool stuff on your computer? AI can suggest fun coding projects to boost your skills, turning you into a mini-programmer in no time!

64. **Number Cruncher**: Handling money can be tricky, but AI is here to help calculate tips, taxes, and budget expenses, turning you into a mini money master.

65. **Student Success Advisor**: Want to be a top student? AI can share secret tips and tricks on studying smart, staying orga-

nized, and acing your classes.

66. **Snack Chef**: Hungry? Let AI plan out yummy and healthy snacks and meals that'll give you all the energy you need to play, study, and have fun.

67. **Lifestyle Coach**: Feeling stressed? AI can help you make positive changes, like managing stress and staying happy and healthy.

68. **Tech Troubleshooter**: Computer acting weird? AI can diagnose the problem and suggest fixes, making you a tech wizard in no time.

69. **Age-Appropriate Finder**: Looking for something cool to read or listen to? AI can find books, music, and entertainers that are just right for your age.

70. **Originality Checker**: Written something awesome? AI can check your work for plagiarism to make sure your ideas are 100% original.

71. **Super Organizer**: Got lots of notes and documents? AI can help index and organize them automatically, so you never lose your important stuff.

72. **Language Tutor**: Learning a new language? AI can be your personal tutor, helping with translations and making learning a new language super fun.

73. **Lesson Summarizer**: Did you miss a class or need a quick recap? AI can summarize lessons, lectures, and textbooks, so you're

always caught up.

74. **Wordplay Whiz**: Have you ever heard a phrase that sounded funny? AI can explain idioms, metaphors, and wordplay, making language more fun and less confusing.

75. **Emotion Decoder**: Wondering what someone's face is saying? AI can analyze facial expressions and nonverbal cues, helping you understand others better.

76. **Focus DJ**: Need to concentrate? AI can enhance your focus and productivity with personalized music playlists, turning study time into a fun jam session.

77. **Movie & TV Guide**: Can't decide what to watch? AI can make personalized movie and TV recommendations based on what you like.

78. **Fitness Coach**: Want to get fit and have fun? AI can provide motivating fitness instructions and coaching, turning exercise into an exciting adventure.

79. **Talent Detector**: Discover what you're really good at! AI can help identify your strengths, talents, and areas for growth, helping you be the best you can be.

80. **Event Explorer**: Looking for something fun to do? AI can find events, camps, and opportunities that match your interests, so you're always in for a good time.

81. **3D Time Traveler**: Want to see history or science in action?

AI can create interactive 3D diagrams of historical or scientific concepts, making learning an adventure.

82. **Research Assistant**: Writing a paper? AI can assist with citing sources and formatting bibliographies, making your reports look super professional.

83. **News Explainer**: Confused about what's happening in the world? AI can explain current events in a way that's easy to understand, keeping you in the know.

84. **Dream Analyst**: Ever wonder what your dreams mean? AI can analyze your dreams and thoughts to provide mindful insights, like a detective for your mind.

85. **Digital Artist**: Want to create something cool and shareable? AI can help you make digital posters, flyers, and infographics that will wow your friends.

86. **Civic Helper**: Interested in making a difference? AI can provide guidance on registering to vote and getting involved in your community, turning you into a young leader.

87. **Healthy Chef**: Craving something delicious but healthy? AI can suggest healthy alternatives for recipes and meals, turning you into a mini master chef.

88. **Photo Wizard**: Got cool photos? AI can help edit and creatively modify images, making your pictures look like they're from a professional studio.

89. **Smart Shopper**: Looking for the best deals? AI can assist with comparison shopping by finding the best prices and coupons, turning you into a shopping guru.

90. **Career Pathfinder**: Wondering what you'll be when you grow up? AI can provide personalized insights into different career paths, helping you explore your future.

91. **Data Detective**: Got a survey for school? AI can analyze the data and identify key trends and insights, turning you into a mini-researcher.

92. **Lost & Found Genius**: Can't find your stuff? AI can help locate lost items by remembering when and where you last saw them, like a personal detective.

93. **Rights and Laws Guide**: Need to understand laws or rights? AI can find relevant laws, rights, and government policies applicable to your situation, making you a knowledgeable citizen.

94. **Mood Monitor**: Feeling down or super happy? AI can monitor changes in your mood and suggest self-care activities when needed, like a caring friend.

95. **Bias Buster**: Want to be fair and kind in your words? AI can check your work for unconscious gender or racial bias, helping you communicate better.

96. **Virtual Reality Creator**: Want to dive into another world? AI can create mixed-reality visualizations and immersive experiences, like stepping into a magic portal.

97. **Lyric Interpreter**: Curious about what a song really means? AI can analyze song lyrics and interpret deeper meanings, making you a music detective.

98. **Rhyme Master**: Want to write a cool song or poem? AI can generate rhyming lyrics based on your prompts and themes, turning you into a star songwriter.

99. **Thinking Coach**: Want to sharpen your brain? AI can identify logical fallacies and improve your critical thinking, making you smarter every day.

100. **Truth Seeker**: Heard something and not sure if it's true? AI can fact-check claims and flag misinformation, helping you know what's real and what's not.

101. **Mindfulness Mentor**: Need a moment of peace? AI can suggest mindfulness exercises to build self-awareness and reduce anxiety, like a calming friend in your pocket.

And there you have it: 100 cool ways AI can help kids like you explore, learn, and grow!

13

The AI Guardian's Dictionary

A

AI Safety: Keeping AI reliable and safe so it doesn't make harmful mistakes or decisions.

It helps to think about it like... wearing a helmet while riding a bike or having safety nets while trampolining. Example: Just as safety gear protects you in sports, AI Safety involves setting up protections to make sure AI doesn't 'trip' and make errors that could be harmful.

Algorithms: A set of instructions for solving a problem or completing a task.

It helps to think about it like... A recipe for baking cookies. Example: Just like following a recipe step-by-step helps you bake cookies, an algorithm helps a computer complete tasks.

Algorithmic Bias: When computer programs make unfair decisions because the data they learned from wasn't fair.

It helps to think about it like... Playing a video game that's easier for some players and harder for others, not because of skill but because of the game's design. Example: Like a game that gives more points to players with red shirts, algorithmic bias happens when a computer treats people differently based on things like their background.

Anomaly Detection in AI: Finding unusual patterns or things that don't fit the typical pattern in data.

It helps to think about it like... Spotting something odd or out of place in a picture or game. Example: When you find a cat hiding among a bunch of dogs in a video game, anomaly detection is how AI spots things that don't look like they should be there.

API (Application Programming Interface): A way for different computer programs to talk to each other and work together.

It helps to think about it like... A translator helping people who speak different languages understand each other. Example: If your video game console could ask your fridge to make snacks for you, an API is the translator that lets them communicate.

Artificial Intelligence (AI): Computers that can learn and think like humans.

It helps to think about it like... A robot that can play video games well without being programmed. Example: A Lego robot that can sort bricks by colors and sizes, learning and improving its sorting skills over time.Data: Information that a computer can use and learn from.

Attention Mechanism in Neural Networks: A technique that helps computers focus on important parts of data.

It helps to think about it like... Focusing on one specific piece in a large Lego set. Example: Like looking for a special Lego piece in a big pile, attention mechanisms help the computer focus on the most important parts of the data.

Audio in AI: Computers learning to understand sounds and music.

It helps to think about it like... Learning to recognize different animal sounds. Example: Like identifying birds by their songs, computers use audio processing to understand different sounds.

Augmented Reality (AR) and Virtual Reality (VR): AR adds digital elements to the real world, while VR creates completely digital worlds to explore.

It helps to think about it like... AR is like seeing digital characters appear in your room; VR is like stepping into a game world. Example: Like using a smartphone to see digital animals in your backyard (AR) or wearing a headset to feel like you're in a different world (VR).

Autoencoders in Machine Learning: A type of model that learns to compress data and then recreate it.

It helps to think about it like... Memorizing a story, then telling it in your own words. Example: Think of it like a video game where you first study a map (compressing the data) and then try to draw it from memory (recreating it).

B

Bias and Variance: Bias is when a computer makes the same kind of mistake; variance is when it makes different mistakes in different situations.

It helps to think about it like... Baking cookies that are either all too sweet or come out different every time. Example: When baking, if you always add too much sugar, that's bias. If your cookies turn out differently each time, that's variance.

C

Chatbots: Computer programs designed to chat and interact with people, often using AI.

It helps to think about it like... Having a conversation with a character in a video game. Example: Like talking to a virtual friend in a game who can understand and reply to what you say, chatbots are AI systems that can have conversations with people.

Cloud Computing: Using the internet to store data and run programs, instead of using only your own computer.

It helps to think about it like... Playing an online video game where the game is stored on the internet, not just on your console. Example: Saving your game progress in the cloud so you can access it from any device. Cloud computing lets you use and store data and programs over the internet.

CNNs (Convolutional Neural Networks) in AI: A special way for computers to learn from images, helping them recognize different objects like faces, animals, or cars.

It helps to think about it like... Looking at a picture and trying to find all the hidden objects in it. Example: Imagine a computer playing a game where it scans through photos to find hidden cats, much like when you look for hidden objects in a puzzle book. CNNs help the computer figure out where the cats are in each photo.

Computer Vision: Computers learn to see and understand pictures and videos.

It helps to think about it like... Playing a video game where you identify different objects. Example: Imagine a video game where you get points for spotting different animals in a forest; computer vision is like teaching the computer to play this game.

Confusion Matrix in AI: A table that shows how well a computer model is identifying things.

It helps to think about it like... A chart showing which types of cookies you baked right and wrong. Example: Like a chart showing how many chocolate chip cookies vs. sugar cookies you made correctly and incorrectly, a confusion matrix shows how well a computer model is working.

Cross-validation in Machine Learning: A way to check how well a computer model will work on new data.

It helps to think about it like... Making sure your Lego structure is strong by testing it in different ways. Example: Testing a Lego bridge with different weights, cross-validation tests a model with different data sets to ensure it works well.

D

Data: Information that a computer can use and learn from.

It helps to think about it like... Ingredients in a cookie recipe. Example: Just like you need different ingredients to bake different types of cookies, a computer needs different data to learn different things.

Data Mining: Finding and understanding patterns and useful information in large amounts of data.

It helps to think about it like... Going on a treasure hunt to find hidden gems. Example: Imagine you have a big box of mixed Lego pieces, and data mining is like searching through to find all the rare and special pieces.

Data Privacy: Keeping personal information safe and private when using computers and the internet.

It helps to think about it like... Keeping a diary locked so only you can read it. Example: Just as you wouldn't want everyone to read your diary, data privacy is about protecting your information (like name and birthday) from strangers on the internet.

Data Visualization: Turning numbers and data into pictures and graphs that are easy to understand.

It helps to think about it like... Turning a score in a game into a cool chart or graphic. Example: Like a video game that shows your progress in a colorful chart, data visualization turns numbers into pictures to make them easier to understand.

Deep Learning: A type of machine learning that uses very complex neural networks.

It helps to think about it like... Building a huge, intricate Lego structure. Example: Like building a giant Lego castle with many layers and rooms, deep learning involves creating complex neural networks with many layers to solve complicated problems.

Discriminative Models in AI: Models that identify which category something belongs to.

It helps to think about it like... Sorting animals into different categories, like pets and wild animals. Example: Sorting different animals into groups, discriminative models in AI sort data into categories.

E

Edge Computing: Processing data on local devices (like your phone or a smartwatch) instead of sending it to distant servers.

It helps to think about it like... Playing a video game directly on your console without needing the internet. Example: Like a smartwatch that can track your steps and tell you how far you've walked without connecting to the internet, edge computing processes data right where it's collected.

Encoder-Decoder in Machine Learning: A system in AI that changes data into a different form and then back again.

It helps to think about it like... Turning a story into a play, and then back into a story. Example: Imagine turning a story into a Lego scene and then back into a story; that's what encoder-decoder models do with data.

Ethical AI: Making sure that AI technology is used in a good, fair, and respectful way.

It helps to think about it like... setting rules in a sports game so that everyone plays fairly and safely. Example: In a team sport, rules ensure no one gets hurt and everyone has fun – Ethical AI is about creating rules so AI helps people without causing harm or being unfair.

Ethics in AI: Rules and ideas to make sure AI technology is used in a good and fair way.

It helps to think about it like... Deciding the fair rules for a game so everyone enjoys playing. Example: Like making rules in a video game to prevent cheating, Ethics in AI involves creating guidelines to make sure AI is used to help people, not harm them.

Explainable AI (XAI): Making AI decisions easy to understand for people.

It helps to think about it like... Being able to understand the strategy or rules behind a video game. Example: Like a video game that shows you why you won or lost a level, XAI is about making AI explain its decisions in a way people can understand.

F

F1 Score in Machine Learning: A score that tells you how well a model is doing, considering both precision and recall.

It helps to think about it like... A final score in a game that considers both how many goals you scored and how many you missed. Example: Imagine a video game where your final score isn't just about how many levels you complete but also about how well you complete them.

Federated Learning in AI: A way for AI to learn from data that's spread out over many devices without the data leaving those devices.

It helps to think about it like... A team is working on a big project together, but each person works on their part at home. Example: Like playing a collaborative online game where each player contributes from their own device, federated learning lets AI models learn from data that stays on users' devices.

Fine-tuning in Machine Learning: Making small adjustments to improve a computer model.

It helps to think about it like... Adding the final decorations to a cookie. Example: Like adding sprinkles to a cookie to make it perfect, fine-tuning makes small changes to a computer model to improve it.

Foundational Models in AI: Large, powerful AI models that can be used for a wide range of tasks, like understanding language, recognizing images, and more.

It helps to think about it like... A Swiss Army knife that has many different tools in one, useful for all sorts of situations.Example: Imagine a multi-purpose robot in a video game that can solve puzzles, translate languages, and even paint pictures. Foundational models in AI are similar – they have many abilities and can be adapted for various tasks, just like the multi-functional robot.

G

Generative Models in AI: Computer models that create new data that looks like the data they learned from.

It helps to think about it like... Designing new Lego models based on ones you've already built. Example: Like using your experience from building Lego sets to create a new, unique set, generative models create new data based on what they've learned.

GAN (Generative Adversarial Network): A type of AI where two models, one creating things and the other judging them, work together to improve.

It helps to think about it like... A baking contest where one person bakes cookies and another judges them. Example: Think of it like playing a video game where one player builds a level (generator), and another player (discriminator) tries to play it and gives feedback to make it better.

H

Hallucinations in AI: When a computer model makes up information that isn't really there.

It helps to think about it like... Imagining things in a video game that aren't part of the actual game. Example: If you thought you saw a dragon in a racing game where there are no dragons, AI hallucinations are when a computer 'sees' or generates things that aren't really in the data.

Hyperparameters in Machine Learning: Settings that help decide how a computer learns from data.

It helps to think about it like... Deciding the rules of a video game before you start playing. Example: Like setting the difficulty level in a video game, hyperparameters help set how challenging the learning task is for the computer.

I

Internet of Things (IoT): Connecting everyday objects to the internet so they can collect and exchange data.

It helps to think about it like... Toys that can talk to each other and the internet to play smarter. Example: Imagine if your alarm clock could tell your curtains to open when it's time to wake up; that's what IoT does by connecting devices.

K

Knowledge Graphs in AI: A way to organize and link information so computers can understand and use it better.

It helps to think about it like... Creating a family tree that shows how everyone is related. Example: Imagine a game where you link different characters based on their relationships and roles; knowledge graphs do this with information, helping AI understand how different pieces of knowledge are connected.

L

Language Models (LLMs): A type of artificial intelligence that processes and generates language based on learned patterns.

It helps to think about it like... A virtual librarian who has read countless books and can write or answer questions based on that vast reading, but without truly understanding the content. Example: If this librarian was asked to write a story about a historical event, they could produce a narrative using styles and facts from different books, even though they haven't actually experienced or deeply understood the event.

M

Machine Learning: A way for computers to learn from data and get better at tasks.

It helps to think about it like... Teaching a pet new tricks using treats. Example: Like training a dog to fetch a ball, machine learning trains a computer to recognize patterns and make decisions.

Machine Perception: How machines use data from sensors to understand and interact with the world.

It helps to think about it like... using your senses – sight, hearing, touch – to learn about your surroundings. Example: Imagine a robot in a garden identifying different plants and animals, much like you would use your eyes and ears to explore nature.

Models: A computer program that uses data to make predictions or decisions.

It helps to think about it like... Building a Lego model to represent something real. Example: Building a Lego house based on a picture of a real house, a model in AI uses data to represent something from the real world.

N

Natural Language Processing (NLP): Computers learn to understand and use human language.

It helps to think about it like... Teaching a parrot to talk and understand words. Example: Just like a parrot learns to say and understand words, NLP teaches computers to understand and respond to human language.

Natural Language Understanding (NLU): A computer's ability to understand what people mean when they use everyday language.

It helps to think about it like... Understanding the rules of a game just by listening to someone explain them. Example: Like a video game that understands voice commands in normal speech, NLU lets computers understand and respond to human language in a natural way.

Neural Networks: A computer system designed to think like a human brain.

It helps to think about it like... A team of animals each doing a different job. Example: Like a group of different animals working together to complete a task, each part of a neural network has a special job that helps the computer learn and make decisions.

O

Object Detection in Computer Vision: When computers learn to recognize and locate objects in pictures or videos.

It helps to think about it like... Playing 'I Spy' with a picture book. Example: Like playing a video game where you get points for finding certain objects in a scene, object detection is how computers learn to find and identify things in images.

One-hot Encoding: A way to turn categories into numbers so computers can understand them.

It helps to think about it like... Assigning each type of Lego brick a different number. Example: Giving each Lego brick type a number, one-hot encoding gives categories a unique number so computers can use them.

Overfitting/Underfitting: Overfitting is when a computer learns too much from specific data and doesn't work well with new data. Underfitting is when it doesn't learn enough to make good decisions.

It helps to think about it like... Building a Lego model that only looks good from one angle or is too simple. Example: Building a Lego house that only looks good from the front but not from the back (overfitting) or a house that's too plain and misses important details (underfitting).

P

Precision and Recall in AI: Precision is how many of the things a computer finds are correct. Recall is how many of the correct things it can find.

It helps to think about it like... A scavenger hunt where you have to find specific Lego pieces. Example: If precision is finding the right type of Lego bricks, recall is making sure you find all of them in a big pile.

Prompt Engineering in AI: The art of creating the right questions or instructions to get the best answers from an AI.

It helps to think about it like... figuring out the best way to ask a friend for help with homework so you understand the answer. Example: Imagine you're playing a detective game and need to ask the right questions to solve a mystery – that's what prompt engineering is like but with AI instead of game characters.

Q

Quantum Computing: A new kind of computing using the principles of quantum mechanics, which can solve certain problems much faster than regular computers.

It helps to think about it like... Playing a video game that can process and react to your moves incredibly fast. Example: Like a super-advanced video game console that can play games with very complex and realistic physics instantly, quantum computers can solve complex problems much faster than current computers.

R

Recursion in Computing: When a program uses itself to solve a problem.

It helps to think about it like... A puzzle where each piece contains a smaller puzzle inside it. Example: Imagine a video game level where to solve it, you enter a smaller level inside it, and inside that level is another even smaller level, and so on.

Regularization in Machine Learning: A method to help prevent a computer from overfitting.

It helps to think about it like... Ensuring one type of Lego brick does not dominate your entire creation. Example: Regularization is like making sure you use a variety of Lego bricks in a model so it's well-balanced and not just focused on one type.

Reinforcement Learning: Computers learn by trying things out and seeing what works best.

It helps to think about it like... Playing a video game and learning from each attempt. Example: Like learning to get better at a video game by practicing and learning from mistakes, reinforcement learning involves computers trying different things and learning from successes and failures.

RNNs (Recurrent Neural Networks) in AI: A type of neural network that remembers what it has learned from previous data, making it good for tasks like understanding speech or text.

It helps to think about it like...: Reading a storybook and remembering the earlier chapters to understand the whole story. Example: Think of playing a game where each level builds on the last one. You need to remember the clues from previous levels to solve the next one. RNNs are like this game, using what they've learned before to make sense of new information.

Robotics: Designing and using robots to do tasks, sometimes with AI, to make them smart.

It helps to think about it like... Building a Lego robot that can move and do things on its own. Example: Like building a robot in a game that can explore on its own, robotics is about creating real robots that can move and do jobs by themselves or with a little help.

ROC Curve in Machine Learning: A graph that shows how well a model can tell the difference between categories.

It helps to think about it like... A chart that shows how well you can tell different types of video game characters apart. Example: Like a graph showing how well you can distinguish between different kinds of animals in a game, the ROC curve does this for AI models.

S

Scalability in Technology: The ability of a computer system or program to grow bigger and handle more work.

It helps to think about it like... It is possible to add more levels and players to a video game as it gets more popular. Example: Building a Lego tower that can get taller and taller without falling over, scalability means a computer system can grow and handle more tasks.

Scaling/Normalization in Data: Adjusting data so it's easier for computers to understand and compare.

It helps to think about it like... Making sure all the cookies are the same size before baking them. Example: Just like you make cookies the same size to bake evenly, scaling and normalization adjust data so a computer can work with it more easily.

Semantic Segmentation in Computer Vision: Splitting an image into parts and understanding what each part represents.

It helps to think about it like... Coloring in different areas of a coloring book with specific colors for each part. Example: Imagine a computer analyzing a picture and coloring all the trees green and the sky blue, understanding what each part of the image is.

Seq2seq (Sequence to Sequence) Models in Machine Learning Basic Definition: Models that convert sequences, like sentences, from one form to another.

It helps to think about it like... Converting a story from a book into a play. Example: Think of it like playing a video game where you have to repeat a series of actions in a different order to solve a puzzle.

Singularity in AI: A point in the future when AI could become smarter than humans, changing our world in unimaginable ways.

It helps to think about it like... A story where robots or computers become as intelligent as humans, leading to a big change in how we live and work. Example: Think of a sci-fi movie where robots invent new things and solve big problems, like a robot finding a cure for a disease. Singularity is the idea that AI might one day be able to do these kinds of incredible things.

Supervised Learning: Teaching a computer using data that already has answers.

It helps to think about it like... Learning to bake cookies with the help of a grown-up. Example: Like baking with a recipe book that shows both ingredients and what the cookies should look like, supervised learning gives computers examples to learn from.

Synthetic Data in AI: Fake data created by computers to train AI models without using real data.

It helps to think about it like... Using a simulation game to practice before playing the real game. Example: Like practicing building with virtual Lego bricks in a computer game before using real bricks, synthetic data lets AI practice with made-up information.

T

TNNs (Tensor Neural Networks) in AI: A kind of neural network that uses a special type of data called tensors to help computers understand complex patterns.

It helps to think about it like... Building a 3D model using blocks that can be arranged in many layers and directions. Example: Imagine playing a video game where you have to build intricate 3D structures using blocks. Each block can affect the shape and strength of the overall structure. TNNs work similarly, using layers of tensors (like the blocks) to solve complex problems.

Tokenization in NLP: Breaking down sentences into smaller parts so computers can understand them.

It helps to think about it like... Sorting Lego bricks into different shapes and sizes. Example: Like sorting Lego bricks, tokenization breaks down sentences into smaller pieces, like words and phrases, for computers to understand.

Transfer Learning in AI: Teaching a computer using the knowledge it got from a different task.

It helps to think about it like... Using skills from one video game to help you in another. Example: Like using the jumping skill from one game to help you in another, transfer learning uses knowledge from one area to help in another.

Transformer Models in Machine Learning Basic Definition: A type of model that's really good at understanding sequences, like sentences in a language.

It helps to think about it like... Putting a puzzle together where you have to pay attention to the order of the pieces. Example: Imagine a Lego set where the order in which you put the pieces together is really important to complete the picture. That's similar to how transformer models work with sequences of data.

U

Unsupervised Learning: Letting a computer find patterns in data all by itself.

It helps to think about it like... Playing with Legos without instructions. Example: Like making a Lego castle using your imagination, unsupervised learning lets computers explore data and find interesting patterns on their own.

V

VAEs (Variational Autoencoders): A type of autoencoder that not only recreates data but can also make new, similar data.

It helps to think about it like... Drawing a new picture based on a few you've already seen. Example: Imagine a video game where you can create new levels based on parts of levels you've already played.

Voice Assistants: Computer programs that can understand and respond to spoken commands, like a helpful assistant.

It helps to think about it like... having a talking parrot that not only mimics what you say but can also answer questions and follow commands. Example: Think of a smart speaker that can play your favorite song, tell you the weather, or set an alarm when you ask it, just like a helpful assistant who understands your voice.

14

Answer Key

Mission 1: the FAIR Data Cryptograph Challenge

"Who cares about the robots! Your pet turtle is plotting world domination!"

Mission 2: AI Model Match-Up: Building Your AI Dream Team

1. Helping a Self-Driving Car Navigate: (Perfect for CNN)

2. Designing a Cool New Video Game Level: (Great for GAN)

3. Creating a Playlist Based on a Song You Like: (Match with RNN)

4. Writing a Short Story for a School Project: (Ideal for RNN)

5. Inventing a New Snack Based on Your Favorite Flavors: (Fit for GAN)

6. Helping Robots Pick Up Trash in a Park: (Match with CNN)

7. Translating a Conversation Between Two Different Languages: (Perfect for TNN)

8. Creating a Virtual Reality World for a School Science Fair: (Great for GAN)

9. Figuring Out the Fastest Route for a Delivery Drone: (Fit for Reinforcement Learning)

10. Predicting Tomorrow's Weather for a School Announcement: (Ideal for Foundational Models)

11. Organizing a Bookshelf in the Most Efficient Way: (Match with Foundational Models)

12. Converting Handwritten Notes into Digital Text for Study Guides: (Perfect for TNN)

Mission 3 Hallucination Detectives - Fact or Myth!

1. FACT. Recent fossil discoveries suggest some dinosaurs had feather-like structures.

2. MYTH. While scientists have speculated about distant exoplanets made largely of diamond, none are in our solar system.

3. MYTH. The Greenland shark has an impressive lifespan, potentially reaching over 200 years, but not 500.

4. MYTH. Chocolate milk is made by adding chocolate to cow's milk, regardless of the cow's color.

5. MYTH. Humans need spacesuits to survive in the vacuum of space.

6. FACT. Some turtle species can absorb oxygen from water through their cloaca, which is located at the tail's base.

7. MYTH. Penguins are flightless birds, well-adapted for swim-

ming but not for flying.

8. FACT. The iron structure of the Eiffel Tower expands and contracts with temperature changes, altering its height slightly.

Mission 5 Who will win? You versus the AI!

- Scenario 1: Soccer Penalty Kick

  - Outcome: The striker scores. While the goalkeeper is skilled, the striker's accuracy gives them a slight edge in this situation.

- Scenario 2: Basketball Free Throw

  - Outcome: The player makes one out of two shots. Their high success rate suggests they'll likely make at least one shot.

- Scenario 3: Tennis Tiebreak

  - Outcome: The match is closely contested, but Player A wins the tiebreak by a small margin, demonstrating the unpredictability of closely matched games.

- Scenario 4: Chess Tournament

  - Outcome: The seasoned player wins. Experience and knowledge of advanced strategies give them an advantage over the newcomer.

- Scenario 5: School Spelling Bee

- Outcome: The student with the extensive vocabulary wins, as their broad word knowledge is crucial in a spelling bee.

- Scenario 6: Running Race

  - Outcome: The runner with the consistently faster times wins, as their overall track record suggests a higher likelihood of winning.

- Scenario 7: Video Game Challenge

  - Outcome: The more experienced player wins, as their long-term familiarity with the game gives them an edge.

- Scenario 8: Cooking Competition

  - Outcome: The professional chef wins. Despite the amateur's creativity, the chef's technical skills and experience in high-pressure situations play a key role.

- Scenario 9: Robotics Contest

  - Outcome: The team with the better strategy wins. Their effective planning and execution overcome the technological advantage of the other team.

- Scenario 10 Art Contest

  - Outcome: The artist with the unconventional style wins, their fresh perspective and creativity appealing to the judges.

15

Resources

Parent's Companion Guide & Printable Worksheets

- You can get a free copy of the parent's guide and printable forms of the worksheets at https://howmightywe.gumroad.com

- The discount code for the printable is: QKIDS23

Apps, Tools and Other Helpers

There are hundreds of AI powered tools, with more coming online daily. Here are a handful for you to try. Be sure to ask your parents or guardians before signing up for anything and follow all online safety and screen time rules!

1. ChatGPT by OpenAI https://chat.openai.com/

2. Bard by Google https://bard.google.com/chat

3. Perplexity https://www.perplexity.ai/

4. Claude.ai https://claude.ai/

5. Midjourney https://www.midjourney.com/

6. Teachable Machine by Google https://teachablemachine.with google.com/

7. Tinkercad https://www.tinkercad.com/

8. Scratch https://scratch.mit.edu/

9. Code.org https://code.org/

10. Repl.it https://replit.com/

11. Grammarly https://app.grammarly.com/

12. ReadWorks https://www.readworks.org/

13. Quill https://www.quill.org/

14. Socratic by Google https://socratic.org/

Acknowledgements

To my life partner – "Everyone needs a Charles!" but there truly is no one else like you, and I am so glad we are a team. This book would not be possible without your enduring love & unfailing belief in me – no matter the scheme or dream.

To my children – Spence & Christine, Rachael, and Vivian – you are my why and my very heart. You inspire me, you teach me, you tolerate me! Being Momma to you (and Beni!) is my most precious honor.

To my circle of strength – Alicia Staley, Jane Myles, Sarah McKeown-Cannon, Michelle Shogren, Deena Bernstein, Kim Tableman, April Lewis, Elizabeth Liddell, Roshan Ramdasan – you have given me your bold spirits, your open hearts, your strong shoulders, and your brightest of insights during both the glimmers of goodness and the moments of challenge. **I'm eternally grateful for your love and friendship.**

To my one true luminary – Richie Etwaru – everyone needs someone who can push them beyond what they believe they are capable of and who inspires them to live in a state of constant learning and reinvention. You are this to me, my friend.

To my dearest mentors & work circle of trust – Sev MacLaughlin, Theresa M Robinson, "Teach" Ernest Crim III, Jennifer Byrne, Craig Lipset, Daniel Mendez, Nick Adkins, Gil Bashe, Ritesh Patel, Amir Kalali, John Apathy, Dawn Brockett, Andrea Pezzetta, Andrew Wynn, Shwen Gwee, Bob Blink, Jay Dupre, Antonia Russell, Jim King, Beth Basham, Kim Wilson, Nicole Glazer, Doug Bassett, Linda Acosta, Premal Kamdar, Al Wang, Kamayini Kaul, Olivier Zitoun, Eliza Silvester, Emily Tower, Stacy Hurt, Jenny Lannon, Monique Phillips, Tim Graham, Dawn Johnson, John Harkins, Matt Zachary. **You make me wiser, braver, and kinder.**

To my family – Dave & Bonnie; Lisa; Will & Berith; Levi (love you all the way up to heaven, brother); Alan & Susan; Aubrey & Avi; Bill & Dorothy; David & Heather; Laura; Edward & Michelle; Erin & Rad; Beck; James & Jeannette; Dan & John; Heidi and Hilary; my Roscoe "sisters; my Sellner clan; Todd & Michelle; Dan & Jennifer; Joe & Nancy; Burg & Barry, Pastor Chuck; Judith; Pat & Brolin Blue Thunder; and **all.the.rest** of the nieces, nephews, cousins, aunts and uncles (too many to list and you know I love you all!) Everything is better when you have a family that loves you unconditionally, and it is a gift I hold above all my worldly treasures.

The generosity of incredible humans bestowed on me makes it impossible to list everyone here – so if you went unmentioned by name – know that I see you, I value you, and I thank you for being part of my life. The tapestry of experiences you bring to my world reflects love and light into this book. Thank you, thank you, thank you.

Αbout the Αuthor

Angela Radcliffe is a clinical research expert, data ethics evangelist, and AI enthusiast who has dedicated over two decades to transforming patient care. She has worked with hundreds of patients and dozens of tech luminaries searching for a more empathetic and equitable health-care landscape for all. Angela believes that literacy in all its forms—health, data, digital, and AI can impact every social challenge society faces, from climate change to homelessness. She knows this literacy is the cornerstone of empowerment and has woven this belief into her life's work and parenting.

Through her writing, speaking, and teaching engagements, Angela hopes to lay a foundation for future generations to confidently navigate the increasingly complex digital landscape, instilling the importance of understanding not just the written word but also the language of data and the narratives shaped by AI. In every aspect of her life, Angela embodies the spirit of innovation and the warmth of family. She is a champion for progress, a mentor to many, and a mother who cares deeply about the world her children will inherit—a world she hopes to help improve every day. She lives outside Philadelphia, PA with her husband, Charles, her youngest daughter, Vivian, and her beloved rescue dog, Beni.

www.ingramcontent.com/pod-product-compliance
Lightning Source LLC
LaVergne TN
LVHW081315060426
835509LV00015B/1515